THE INFORMAL ESSAY

THE
INFORMAL ESSAY

Edited by PAUL A. JORGENSEN

UNIVERSITY OF CALIFORNIA AT LOS ANGELES

and FREDERICK B. SHROYER

LOS ANGELES STATE COLLEGE

W · W · NORTON & COMPANY · INC · *New York*

Library of Congress Catalog Card No. 61-9155

W. W. Norton & Company, Inc., is also the publisher of *The American Tradition in Literature*, edited by Sculley Bradley, Richmond C. Beatty, and E. Hudson Long; *World Masterpieces*, edited by Maynard Mack, Kenneth Douglas, Howard E. Hugo, Bernard M. W. Knox, John C. McGalliard, P. M. Pasinetti, and René Wellek; *Masterpieces of the Orient*, edited by G. L. Anderson; and other fine anthologies.

PRINTED IN THE UNITED STATES OF AMERICA

2 3 4 5 6 7 8 9 0

CONTENTS

6

ACKNOWLEDGMENTS

To Judith W. Albaum and Jill Macklem the editors are indebted for substantial assistance in the preparation of the manuscript. From Professor William D. Templeman, of the University of Southern California, we have received wise counsel and encouragement. Many others have suggested the need for a book such as this, and we hope that the finished product will at least partially justify the interest and help of all who have contributed to its realization.

INTRODUCTION

Like love, the Informal (or Familiar) Essay can seemingly be defined and described by anyone—until the attempt is made. Then suddenly the type becomes elusive as a vagrant summer breeze.

Nevertheless, there are some qualities that can be isolated and examined. *Intimacy* is probably a key word in any attempt at definition. The Informal Essay may be considered as a prose counterpart of the relaxed, often discursive talk of good friends who—moving in a climate of mutual respect and secure in their knowledge of each other's likes, dislikes, crotchets, and interests —find it unnecessary to encumber their interchanges with formalities.

It is noticeable that the pronoun "I" is conspicuously present in many Informal Essays. Again one thinks of the intimacy that surrounds the conversations of friends. Or, to come closer to the Informal Essay itself, one may think of the spoken monologue that anticipates the questions and the thoughts of the listener to such effect that though only one person is speaking, the other by his receptivity and empathy is a very real, however silent, partner in what is occurring.

Similarly, the writer of the Informal Essay drops all pretenses; he comes to the reader dressed in old clothes and wearing scuffed but comfortable shoes. He slouches in his favorite chair and leans toward the reader. Then the writer of the Informal Essay begins to talk. Sometimes he speaks with the easy informative affability of one who has been someplace the reader

9

has not; sometimes he speaks of experiences they have shared. His conversation may start with a casual comment about a recent baseball game or a current political contest. Superficially, what follows may seem a random outpouring without obvious form or direction. But under the carefully selected words of the good essayist, a tone is established that, moving beneath shifting surfaces, conveys coherent and meaningful criticism, knowledge, and speculation. Indeed, although often apparently characterized by lightness and sprightliness, the Informal Essay may smoothly and imperceptibly take as its domain the most significant and serious matters of human life.

This casualness, this lightness, is the product of a great skill drawing upon intelligence. It also derives from the writer's awareness that the really important things of life are too deep to be framed by formalism, pretensions, and syntactical affectations. The master of the Informal Essay has learned that the most difficult attainment of the writer is the ability to write simply—and yet, within that simplicity, to say directly and well everything that he wants to say.

As one continues to attempt to define the Informal Essay, he finds that the word *humor* continually presents itself, demanding that it be utilized in the definition. Certainly humor is often an element, if not a key mood, of the Informal Essay. But this matter of humor is not as simple as it may first appear. Perennial jests and comic euphemisms surround the subjects of death, disaster, and love in all of its physical manifestations; but this humorous embroidery is not woven from a belief that such matters are unimportant. Indeed, we are all instinctively aware that they are the most important realities in our lives; but if we think further about it, we realize that the humor which sometimes accompanies the contemplation of these serious matters brings not only relief from their implications, but also a deeper understanding which permits us to adjust to their implacabilities.

It is not, then, enough to say that the Informal Essay is often humorous and let it go at that. Humor in the Informal Essay is often a vehicle for serious criticism, meaningful commentary, and speculation about the very essentials of life.

We may with profit seek to contrast the Informal Essay with the Formal Essay. We soon discover that a twilight, merging zone exists in which they flow together. But if we disregard this area, several differences may be noted. We have already suggested some of these; but perhaps the most important difference is that the Formal Essay is mainly factual, informative, and argumentative, and as such is limited to a factual, intellectual exposition of precise areas. At its best it is exact and totally clear. The Informal Essay, on the other hand, has no such limitations. It is creative and eclectic; its subject matter can be manipulated so that it becomes related to the larger, sometimes total, human experience. The informal essayist is free to wander off into the future or to the farthest star. He may discuss a bird and in doing so say something about man and machines; or he may discuss a fishless pool and in the process comment significantly upon the nature of man.

One might even suggest that the Formal Essay is essentially scientific and inductive in its approach, while the Informal Essay—though it can easily be as logical as the Formal Essay—is usually more speculative, exploratory, and far-ranging in its treatment of its materials. Too, in the matter of tone and attitude, the writer of the Formal Essay speaks as an authority who is explicating his subject to those who know less about it than he does, while the author of the Informal Essay, it may be pointed out again, speaks, at least apparently, as an equal to equals.

Finally, the Informal Essay bridges the "factual" and the "imaginative." It is probable that the Informal Essay best meets the admittedly ambiguous standards of "literature." Felicity of phrase, precision of word selection, the use of poetic and emotive imagery, symphonic intellectual and emotional patterns, unfettered awareness of the broad texture of all human experience and of the infinite threads with which it is woven, and the sensitivity of the artist—all are the substances upon which the writer of the Informal Essay can, and at his best does, draw.

The Informal Essay then, although ultimately undefinable, exists as a rich literary form. If one cannot define it precisely, he can feel what it is. And that, perhaps, is the best kind of definition, anyway.

THE INFORMAL ESSAY

NO ESSAYS—PLEASE!

Joseph Wood Krutch

*Joseph Wood Krutch (1893–   ), critic and essayist, has few
equals in the field of drama criticism and the more general area
of philosophic and contemplative essays. He is distinguished not
only as a writer, but also as a teacher; he has held the positions of
Professor of Journalism and Professor of Dramatic Literature at
Columbia University.*

*The following essay shows that he is equally skilled in the in-
formal, familiar essay. The essay captures both the attitude and
the subject which Krutch himself postulates: humorous, but not
funny; dignified, but not staid; and an approach to a subject which
is neither momentous nor silly, but somewhere in between.*

*In 1950, after retiring from being drama critic of Nation, and
teaching at Columbia, he went to live in the Arizona desert, where
he has continued his interest in nature. His major works include*
Comedy and Conscience After the Restoration (1924) *and* The
Modern Temper (1929).

Every now and then someone regrets publicly the passing of the
familiar essay. Perhaps such regretters are usually in possession
of a recent rejection slip; in any event there are not enough of
them to impress editors. The very word "essay" has fallen into
such disfavor that it is avoided with horror and anything which
is not fiction is usually called either an "article," a "story" or
just "a piece." When *The Atlantic Monthly*, once the last re-
fuge of a dying tradition, now finds it advisable to go in for
such "articles" as its recent "What Night Playing Has Done to
Baseball" it is obvious that not merely the genteel tradition but
a whole literary form is dead.

I am sure that the books on how to become a writer in ten

easy lessons have been stressing this fact for a long time now. If *I* were writing such a book I certainly should, and I think that I could give some very practical advice. To begin with I should say something like the following:

Suppose that you have drawn a subject out of your mental box and you find that it is "Fish." Now if you were living in the time of Henry Van Dyke and Thomas Bailey Aldrich your best lead would be: "Many of my friends are ardent disciples of Izaak Walton." That would have had the appropriate personal touch and the requisite, not too recondite literary allusion. But today of course no live-wire editor would read any further, not because this sounds like a dull familiar essay but simply because it sounds like a familiar essay. But "Fish" is still a perfectly usable subject provided you remember that salable non-fiction "pieces" almost invariably fall into one of three categories: the factual, the polemic, and what we now call—though I don't know why we have to deviate into French—*reportage*.

If you decide to be factual a good beginning would be: "Four million trout flies were manufactured last year by the three leading sports-supply houses." That is the sort of thing which makes almost any editor sit up and take notice. But it is no better than certain other possible beginnings. The polemic article ought to start: "Despite all the efforts of our department of wild life conservation, the number of game fish in American lakes and streams continues to decline steadily." Probably this kind of beginning to this kind of article is best of all because it sounds alarming and because nowadays (and for understandable reasons) whatever sounds alarming is generally taken to be true. However, if you want to go in for the trickier *reportage* start off with a sentence something like this: " 'Cap' Bill Hanks, a lean, silent, wryly humorous down-Easterner probably knows more about the strange habits of the American fisherman than any man alive."

Of course no one will ever inquire where you got your statistics about the trout flies, whether the fish population really is declining, or whether 'Cap' Bill Hanks really exists. In fact one of the best and lengthiest "Profiles" *The New Yorker* ever ran turned out to be about a "character" at the Fulton Fishmarket who didn't. Whatever looks like official fact or on-the-spot reporting is taken at face value and will be widely quoted. The important thing is that the editor first and the reader afterwards shall get the feeling that what he is being offered is not mere literature but the real lowdown on something or other—whether that something or other is or is not anything he cares much about.

Fling your facts around, never qualify anything (qualifications arouse distrust), and adopt an air of jolly omniscience. Remember that "essays" are written by introverts, "articles" by extroverts, and that the reader is going to resent anything which comes between him and that lowdown which it is your principal function to supply. "Personalities," the more eccentric the better, are fine subjects for *reportage*. Manufacture or get hold of a good one and you may be able to do a "profile." But no one wants any personality to show in the magazine writer, whose business it is to be all-knowing, shrewd, and detached almost to the point of nonexistence. This means of course that your style should have no quality which belongs to you, only the qualities appropriate to the magazine for which you are writing. The most successful of all the magazines functioning in America today seldom print anything which is not anonymous and apparently owe a considerable part of their success to that fact that nearly everything which appears in them achieves the manner of *Life*, *Time*, or *Fortune*, as the case may be, but never by any chance any characteristic which would enable the most sensitive analyst of style to discover who had written it.

The ideal is obviously a kind of writing which seems to have been produced not by a man but by some sort of electronic machine. Perhaps in time it will actually be produced that way, since such machines now solve differential equations and that is harder to do than to write the average magazine article. Probably if Vannevar Bush were to put his mind to the problem he could replace the whole interminable list of editors, assistant editors, and research assistants employed by the Luce publications with a contraption less elaborate than that now used to calculate the trajectory of a rocket. Meanwhile the general effect of mechanical impersonality can be achieved by a system of collaboration in the course of which such personalities as the individual collaborators may have are made to cancel one another out.

This system works best when these collaborators are divided into two groups called respectively "researchers" and "writers" —or, in other words, those who know something but don't write and those who don't know anything but do. This assures at the very outset that the actual writers shall have no dangerous interest in or even relation to what they write and that any individuality of approach which might tend to manifest itself in one of them will be canceled out by the others. If you then pass the end-result through the hands of one or more senior editors for further regularization you will obviously get finally something from which every trace of what might be called handwork has disappeared. One might suppose that the criticism of the arts would be a department in which some trace of individuality would still be considered desirable, but I am reliably informed that at least at one time (and for all I know still) it was the custom to send an "editor" along with the movie critic to see every film so that this editor could tell the critic whether or not the film should be reviewed. This disposed of the possibility that the review might in some way reflect the critic's taste.

Obviously, few publications can afford the elaborate machinery which the Luce organization has set up. However, a great many strive to achieve something of the same effect by simpler means and they expect their contributors to co-operate by recognizing the ideal and by coming as close to the realization of it as is possible for an individual to come. The circulations achieved by these publications seem to indicate how wise from one point of view their policy is. Those which still permit or even encourage a certain amount of individuality in their writers, even those which still offer a certain amount of non-fiction which is to some extent personal and reflective as opposed to the factual and the bleaky expository—must content themselves with relatively small circulations. Moreover, since they also print a good deal of the other sort of thing they create the suspicion that they survive in spite of rather than because of their limited hospitality to the man-made as opposed to the machine-made article.

No doubt the kind of essay which *The Atlantic* and the old *Century* once went in for died of anemia. It came to represent the genteel tradition at its feeblest. No one need be surprised that it did not survive. But what is significant is the fact that whereas the genteel novel was succeeded by novels of a different sort and genteel poetry by poetry in a different manner, the familiar essay died without issue so that what disappeared was a once important literary form for which changed times found no use. And the result is that there disappeared with it the best opportunity to consider in an effective way an area of human interest.

Because the "article" is impersonal it can deal only with subjects which exist in an impersonal realm. If its subject is not ominous, usually it must be desperately trivial; and just as the best-selling books are likely to have for title either something like "The World in Crisis" or "My Grandmother Did a Strip Tease," so the magazine articles which are not heavy are very likely to be inconsequential. I doubt that anyone was ever quite as eccentric as almost every subject of a *New Yorker* profile is made to seem; but if a topic cannot be made "devastating" the next best thing is to treat it as "fabulous."

Perhaps what disappeared with the familiar essay was not merely a form, not merely even an attitude but a whole subject matter. For the familiar essay affords what is probably the best method of discussing those subjects which are neither obviously momentous nor merely silly. And since no really good life is composed exclusively of problems and farce either the reading of most people today does not actually concern itself with some of the most important aspects of their lives or those lives are impoverished to a degree which the members of any really civilized society would find it difficult to understand. Just as genuine conversation—by which I mean something distinguishable from disputation, lamentation, and joke-telling—has tended to disappear from social gatherings, so anything comparable to it has tended to disappear from the printed page. By no means all of the Most-of-My-Friends essays caught it. But the best of them caught something which nowadays hardly gets into print at all.

Somehow we have got into the habit of assuming that even the so-called "human problems" are best discussed in terms as inhuman as possible. Just how one can profitably consider dispassionately so passionate a creature as man I do not know, but that seems to be the enterprise to which we have committed ourselves. The magazines are full of articles dealing statistically with, for example, the alleged failure or success of marriage. Lawyers discuss the law, sociologists publish statistics, and psychologists discuss case histories. Those are the methods by which we deal with the behavior of animals since animals can't talk. But men can—or at least once could—communicate, and one man's "familiar essay" on love and marriage might get closer to some all important realities than any number of "studies" could.

No one is, to take another example, naive enough to suppose that all the current discussions of the welfare state are actually as "objective" as most of them pretend to be. Personal tastes, even simple self-interest, obviously influence most of them, but only insofar as they introduce distortions between the lines. Everybody who writes for or against the competitive society tries to write as though he did not live in it, had had no personal experience of what living in it is like, and was dealing only with a question in which he had no personal interest. This is the way one talks about how to keep bees or raise the Black Angus. It is not the way either the bees or the Black Angus would discuss the good life as it affected them, and it is a singularly unrealistic way of considering anything which would affect us. Even the objective studies would be better and more objective if their authors permitted themselves freely to express elsewhere their "familiar" reaction to conditions and prospects, instead of working these feeling in diguised as logical argument or scientific deduction.

All the sciences which deal with man have a tendency to depersonalize him for the simple reason that they tend to disregard everything which a particular science cannot deal with. Just as medicine confessedly deals with the physical man and economics confessedly deals not with Man but with the simplification officially designated as The Economic Man, so psychiatry deals with a fictitious man of whom there would be nothing more to be said if he were "normal," and one branch of psychology deals with what might be called the I-Q man whose only significant aspect is his ability to solve puzzles.

Literature is the only thing which deals with the whole complex phenomenon at once, and if all literature were to cease to exist the result would probably be that in the end whatever is not considered by one or another of the sciences would no longer be taken into account at all and would perhaps almost cease to exist. The Man would no longer be—or at least no longer be observed to be—anything different from the mechanical sum of the Economic man, the I.Q. man, and the other partial men with whom the various partial sciences deal. Faced with that prospect we may well look with dismay at the disappearance of any usable literary form and wonder whether or not we have now entered upon a stage during which man's lingering but still complex individuality finds itself more and more completely deprived of the opportunity not only to express itself in living but even to discover corresponding individualities revealing themselves in the spoken or the written word.

That the situation could be radically altered by the cultivation of the familiar essay I am hardly prepared to maintain. Its disappearance is only a minor symptom. Or perhaps it is just a little bit more than that. At least there are a number of subjects which might profitably be discussed by fewer experts and more human beings. They might achieve a different kind of understanding of certain problems and they might lead to more humanly acceptable conclusions. "Most of my friends seem to feel that . . ."

OF AGE

Michel de Montaigne

*Michel Eyquem de Montaigne (1533–1592), French philosopher
and essayist, was a writer who made doubt a legitimate philosophical
concept. His famous motto was "Que sais-je?" ("What do I
know?") It was substantially his habit of quizzical introspection,
combined with a patiently meditative mind, that enabled him to
become the first and foremost of personal essayists. Previous prose
writers had written mostly about the world around them, only occasionally examining life from the vantage points of their own sensations, weaknesses, and acknowledged prejudices. Montaigne not
only revealed through his own gropings a sensitive and vivacious
mind; he also pointed the future for the Informal Essay by demon-
strating that when an interesting mind lays itself bare, it also lays
bare much of the nature of all men.*

I cannot accept the way in which we establish the duration of
our life. I see that the sages, as compared with popular opinion,
make it a great deal shorter. "What," said the younger Cato[1]
to those who wanted to keep him from killing himself, "am
I now at an age where I can be reproached for abandoning life
too soon?" Yet he was only forty-eight. He regarded that age
as quite ripe and quite advanced, considering how few men
reach it. And those who delude themselves with the idea that
some course or other which they call natural promises a few
years beyond, might do so properly if they had a privilege to
exempt them from the many accidents to which we are all

[1] Marcus Porcius Cato (95–46 B.C.) was a Roman Stoic philosopher.

22

naturally subject, and which can interrupt this course that they promise themselves.

What an idle fancy it is to expect to die of a decay of powers brought on by extreme old age, and to set ourselves this term for our duration, since that is the rarest of all deaths and the least customary! We call it alone natural, as if it were contrary to nature to see a man break his neck by a fall, be drowned in a shipwreck, or be snatched away by the plague or a pleurisy, and as if our ordinary condition did not expose us to all these mishaps. Let us not flatter ourselves with these fine words: we ought perhaps rather to call natural what is general, common, and universal.

Death of old age is a rare, singular, and extraordinary death, and hence less natural than the others; it is the last and ultimate sort of death; the further it is from us, the less it is to be hoped for. It is indeed the bourn beyond which we shall not go, and which the law of nature has prescribed as not to be passed; but it is a very rare privilege of hers to make us last that long. It is an exemption which she grants by special favor to a single person in the space of two or three centuries, relieving him of the misfortunes and difficulties that she has cast in the way of others during this long period.

Thus my idea is to consider the age we have reached as one few people reach. Since in the ordinary course of things men do not come thus far, it is a sign that we are well along. And since we have passed the customary limits which are the true measure of our life, we must not hope to go much further. Having escaped so many occasions of dying, at which we see everyone stumble, we must recognize that an extraordinary fortune, and one out of the usual, like the one that is keeping us going, is not due to last much longer.

It is a defect in the very laws to hold this false idea: they have it that a man is not capable of the management of his estate until he is twenty-five, whereas he will hardly keep the management of his life that long. Augustus[2] cut off five years

---

[2] This title, "Augustus," meaning *sacred*, was conferred upon Gaius Octavius, the first Roman emperor (63 B.C.–14 A.D.).

from the ancient Roman ordinances, and declared that it was
enough for those assuming the office of judge to be thirty.
Servius Tullius[3] released the knights who had passed forty-seven
from service in war; Augustus set this back to forty-five. To send
men back into retirement before the age of fifty-five or sixty
seems not very reasonable to me. I should be of the opinion
that our employment and occupation should be extended as
far as possible, for the public welfare; I find the fault in the
other direction, that of not putting us to work soon enough.
Augustus had been universal judge of the world at nineteen, and
yet would have a man be thirty in order to pass judgement on
the position of a gutter.

As for me, I think our souls are as developed at twenty as
they are ever to be, and give the promise of all they ever can do.
No soul which at that age has not given very evident earnest
of its strength has given proof of it later. The natural qualities
and virtues give notice within that term, or never, of whatever
vigor or beauty they possess:

> If the thorn will not prick at birth,
> It never will prick on earth,

they say in Dauphiné.

If I were to enumerate all the beautiful human actions, of
whatever kind, that have come to my knowledge, I should think
I would find that the greater part were performed, both in
ancient times and in our own, before the age of thirty, rather
than after. Yes, often even in the lives of the same men.

May I not say that with all assurance about those of Hannibal[4] and of Scipio,[5] his great adversary? They lived a good
half of their life on the glory acquired in their youth: great
men afterward in comparison with all others, but by no means
in comparison with themselves.

[3] Legendary king of the Romans (578–534 B.C.).
[4] Hannibal (247–183 B.C.) was a Carthaginian general renowned for
his undying hatred of Rome. After his final defeat by Roman forces, he
killed himself.
[5] Scipio Africanus, known as Scipio the Elder (237–183 B.C.), who
defeated Hannibal at the Battle of Zama (202 B.C.).

As for me, I hold it as certain that since that age my mind and my body have rather shrunk than grown, and gone backward rather than forward. It is possible that in those who employ their time well, knowledge and experience grow with living; but vivacity, quickness, firmness, and other qualities much more our own, more important and essential, wither and languish.

> When age has crushed the body with its might,
> The limbs collapse with weakness and decay,
> The judgment limps, and mind and speech give way.

Sometimes it is the body that first surrenders to age, sometimes, too, it is the mind; and I have seen enough whose brains were enfeebled before their stomach and legs; and inasmuch as this is a malady hardly perceptible to the sufferer and obscure in its symptoms, it is all the more dangerous. For the time, I complain of the laws, not that they leave us at work too long, but that they set us to work too late. It seems to me that considering the frailty of our life and how many ordinary natural reefs it is exposed to, we should not allot so great a part of it to birth, idleness, and apprenticeship.

HINTS TOWARD AN ESSAY
ON CONVERSATION

Jonathan Swift

Jonathan Swift (1667–1745), essayist and satirist, is best known for Gulliver's Travels, *a biting satire on the weakness and ridiculousness of mankind. Misanthrope though he was, he was also deeply aware of the injustices of his age, especially those involving the economic and political interests of Ireland.*

The following essay shows Swift's cunning wit, his astute observations, and his precise details which give to his writing a vivacity found in the Informal Essay only at its best.

I have observed few obvious subjects to have been so seldom, or at least so slightly, handled as this; and indeed I know few so difficult to be treated as it ought, nor yet, upon which there seems so much to be said.

Most things pursued by men for the happiness of public or private life, our wit or folly have so refined that they seldom subsist but in idea; a true friend, a good marriage, a perfect form of government, with some others, require so many ingredients, so good in their several kinds, and so much niceness in mixing them, that for some thousands of years men have despaired of reducing their schemes to perfection; but in conversation it is or might be otherwise; for here we are only to avoid a multitude of errors, which, although a matter of some difficulty, may be in every man's power, for want of which it remains as mere an idea as the other. Therefore, it seems to me that the truest way to understand conversation is to know the faults and errors to which it is subject, and from thence every man to form maxims to himself whereby it may be regu-

[*From Volume X of Swift's* Works, *Dublin, 1763, 163–177.*]

lated, because it requires few talents to which most men are not born, or at least may not acquire without any great genius or study. For nature has left every man a capacity of being agreeable, though not of shining in company; and there are a hundred men sufficiently qualified for both, who, by a very few faults, that they might correct in half an hour, are not so much as tolerable.

I was prompted to write my thoughts upon this subject by mere indignation, to reflect that so useful and innocent a pleasure, so fitted for every period and condition of life, and so much in all men's power, should be so much neglected and abused.

And in this discourse it will be necessary to note those errors that are obvious, as well as others which are seldomer observed, since there are few so obvious or acknowledged into which most men, some time or other, are not apt to run.

For instance, nothing is more generally exploded than the folly of talking too much; yet I rarely remember to have seen five people together, where some one among them has not been predominant in that kind, to the great constraint and disgust of all the rest. But among such as deal in multitudes of words, none are comparable to the sober, deliberate talker, who proceeds with much thought and caution, makes his preface, branches out into several digressions, finds a hint that puts him in mind of another story, which he promises to tell you when this is done; comes back regularly to his subject, cannot readily call to mind some person's name, holding his head, complains of his memory; the whole company all this while in suspense; at length says it is no matter, and so goes on. And, to crown the business, it perhaps proves at last a story the company has heard fifty times before; or, at best, some insipid adventure of the relater.

Another general fault in conversation is that of those who affect to talk of themselves; some, without any ceremony, will run over the history of their lives; will relate the annals of their diseases, with the several symptoms and circumstances of them; will enumerate the hardships and injustice they have suffered in court, in parliament, in love, or in law. Others are more dexterous, and with great art will lie on the watch to hook in their own praise; they will call a witness to remember they always foretold what would happen in such a case, but none would believe them; they advised such a man from the beginning, and told him the consequences, just as they happened, but he would have his own way. Others make a vanity of telling their faults; they are the strangest men in the world; they cannot dissemble; they own it is a folly; they have lost abundance of advantages by it; but, if you would give them the world, they cannot help it; there is something in their nature that abhors insincerity and constraint—with many other insufferable topics of the same altitude.

Of such mighty importance every man is to himself, and ready to think he is so to others, without once making this easy and obvious reflection, that his affairs can have no more weight with other men than theirs have with him; and how little that is, he is sensible enough.

Where a company has met, I often have observed two persons discover, by some accident, that they were bred together at the same school or university; after which the rest are condemned to silence, and to listen while these two are refreshing each other's memory with the arch tricks and passages of themselves and their comrades.

I know a great officer of the army who will sit for some time with a supercilious and impatient silence, full of anger and contempt for those who are talking; at length, of a sudden, demand audience, decide the matter in a short, dogmatical way; then withdraw within himself again, and vouchsafe to talk no more until his spirits circulate again to the same point.

There are some faults in conversation which none are so subject to as the men of wit, nor ever so much as when they are with each other. If they have opened their mouths without endeavouring to say a witty thing, they think it is so many words lost: it is a torment to the hearers, as much as to themselves, to see them upon the rack for invention, and in perpetual constraint, with so little success. They must do something extraordinary in order to acquit themselves and answer their character, else the standers-by may be disappointed, and be apt to think them only like the rest of mortals. I have known two men of wit industriously brought together, in order to entertain the company, where they have made a very ridiculous figure and provided all the mirth at their own expense.

I know a man of wit who is never easy but where he can be allowed to dictate and preside; he neither expects to be informed or entertained, but to display his own talents. His business is to be good company, and not good conversation; and therefore he chooses to frequent those who are content to listen and profess themselves his admirers. And, indeed, the worst conversation I ever remember to have heard in my life was that at Will's coffee-house, where the wits (as they were called) used formerly to assemble; that is to say, five or six men who had writ plays, or at least prologues, or had a share in a miscellany, came thither and entertained one another with their trifling composures, in so important an air as if they had been the noblest efforts of human nature, or that the fate of kingdoms depended on them; and they were usually attended with an humble audience of young students from the inns of court or the universities, who at due distance listened to these oracles, and returned home with great contempt for their law and philosophy, their heads filled with trash under the name of politeness, criticism, and *belles-lettres*.

By these means, the poets, for many years past, were all overrun with pedantry. For, as I take it, the word is not properly used, because pedantry is the too frequent or unseasonable obtruding our own knowledge in common discourse, and placing too great a value upon it; by which definition, men of the court or the army may be as guilty of pedantry as a philosopher or a divine; and it is the same vice in women, when they are over copious upon the subject of their petticoats, or their fans, or their china. For which reason, although it be a piece of prudence as well as good manners to put men upon talking on subjects they are best versed in, yet that is a liberty a wise man could hardly take, because, beside the imputation of pedantry, it is what he would never improve by.

The great town is usually provided with some player, mimic, or buffoon, who has a general reception at the good tables; familiar and domestic with persons of the first quality, and usually sent for at every meeting to divert the company— against which I have no objection. You go there as to a farce or a puppetshow; your business is only to laugh in season, either out of inclination or civility, while this merry companion is acting his part. It is a business he has undertaken, and we are to suppose he is paid for his day's work. I only quarrel when, in select and private meetings, where men of wit and learning are invited to pass an evening, this jester should be admitted to run over his circle of tricks and make the whole company unfit for any other conversation, beside the indignity of confounding men's talents at so shameful a rate.

Raillery is the finest part of conversation; but, as it is our usual custom to counterfeit and adulterate whatever is too dear for us, so we have done with this, and turned it all into what is generally called repartee, or being smart; just as when an expensive fashion comes up, those who are not able to reach it, content themselves with some paltry imitation. It now passes for raillery to run a man down in discourse, to put him out of countenance and make him ridiculous; sometimes to expose the defects of his person or understanding; on all which occasions he is obliged not to be angry, to avoid the imputation of not being able to take a jest. It is admirable to observe one who is dexterous at this art of singling out a weak adversary, getting the laugh on his side, and then carrying all before him. The French, from whence we borrow the word, have a quite different idea of the thing, and so had we in the politer age of our fathers. Raillery was to say something that at first appeared a reproach or reflection, but by some turn of wit, unexpected and surprising, ended always in a compliment, and to the advantage of the person it was addressed to. And surely one of the best rules in conversation is, never say a thing which any of the company can reasonably wish we had rather left unsaid; nor can there anything be well more contrary to the ends for which people meet together than to part unsatisfied with each other or themselves.

There are two faults in conversation which appear very different, yet arise from the same root and are equally blameable; I mean an impatience to interrupt others, and the uneasiness of being interrupted ourselves. The two chief ends of conversation are to entertain and improve those we are among, or to receive those benefits ourselves; which whoever will consider, cannot easily run into either of these two errors; because, when any man speaks in company, it is to be supposed he does it for his hearers' sake, and not his own; so that common discretion will teach us not to force their attention, if they are not willing to lend it; nor, on the other side, to interrupt him who is in possession, because that is in the grossest manner to give the preference to our own good sense.

There are some people whose good manners will not suffer them to interrupt you, but, what is almost as bad, will discover abundance of impatience and lie upon the watch until you have done, because they have started something in their own thoughts which they long to be delivered of. Meantime, they are so far from regarding what passes that their imaginations are wholly turned upon what they have in reserve, for fear it should slip out of their memory; and thus they confine their invention, which might otherwise range over a hundred things full as good, and that might be much more naturally introduced.

There is a sort of rude familiarity which some people, by practicing among their intimates, have introduced into their general conversation, and would have it pass for innocent freedom or humour; which is a dangerous experiment in our northern climate, where all the little decorum and politeness we have are purely forced by art, and are so ready to lapse into barbarity. This, among the Romans, was the raillery of slaves, of which we have many instances in Plautus.[1] It seems to have

---

[1] Titus Maccius Plautus (254?–184 B.C.) was a Roman dramatist.

been introduced among us by Cromwell, who by preferring the scum of the people made it a court entertainment, of which I have heard many particulars; and, considering all things were turned upside down, it was reasonable and judicious; although it was a piece of policy found out to ridicule a point of honour in the other extreme, when the smallest word misplaced among gentlemen ended in a duel.

There are some men excellent at telling a story, and provided with a plentiful stock of them, which they can draw out upon occasion in all companies; and, considering how low conversation runs now among us, it is not altogether a contemptible talent; however, it is subject to two unavoidable defects, frequent repetition, and being soon exhausted; so that whoever values this gift in himself has need of a good memory, and ought frequently to shift his company, that he may not discover the weakness of his fund; for those who are thus endowed have seldom any other revenue, but live upon the main stock.

Great speakers in public are seldom agreeable in private conversation, whether their faculty be natural, or acquired by practice and often venturing. Natural elocution, although it may seem a paradox, usually springs from a barrenness of invention and of words; by which men who have only one stock of notions upon every subject and one set of phrases to express them in, they swim upon the superficies and offer themselves on every occasion; therefore, men of much learning, and who know the compass of a language, are generally the worst talkers on a sudden, until much practice has inured and emboldened them; because they are confounded with plenty of matter, variety of notions and of words, which they cannot readily choose, but are perplexed and entangled by too great a choice; which is no disadvantage in private conversation, where, on the other side, the talent of haranguing is, of all others, most unsupportable.

Nothing has spoiled men more for conversation than the character of being wits; to support which, they never fail of encouraging a number of followers and admirers, who list themselves in their service, wherein they find their accounts on both sides by pleasing their mutual vanity. This has given the former such an air of superiority, and made the latter so pragmatical, that neither of them are well to be endured. I say nothing here of the itch of dispute and contradiction, telling of lies, or of those who are troubled with the disease called the wandering of the thoughts, that they are never present in mind at what passes in discourse; for whoever labours under any of these possessions is as unfit for conversation as a madman in Bedlam.

I think I have gone over most of the errors in conversation that have fallen under my notice or memory, except some that are merely personal, and others too gross to need exploding, such as lewd or profane talk; but I pretend only to treat the errors of conversation in general, and not the several subjects of discourse, which would be infinite. Thus we see how human nature is most debased by the abuse of that faculty which is held the greatest distinction between men and brutes, and how little advantage we make of that which might be the greatest, the most lasting, and the most innocent as well as useful pleasure of life; in default of which we are forced to take up with those poor amusements of dress and visiting, or the more pernicious ones of play, drink, and vicious amours; whereby the nobility and gentry of both sexes are entirely corrupted both in body and mind, and have lost all notions of love, honour, friendship, generosity; which, under the name of fopperies, have been for some time laughed out of doors.

This degeneracy of conversation, with the pernicious consequences thereof upon our humours and dispositions, has been owing, among other causes, to the custom arisen, for some time past, of excluding women from any share in our society, farther than in parties at play, or dancing, or in the pursuit of an amour. I take the highest period of politeness in England (and it is of the same date in France) to have been the peaceable part of King Charles the First's reign; and from what we read of those times, as well as from the accounts I have formerly met with from some who lived in that court, the methods then used for raising and cultivating conversation were altogether different from ours: several ladies, whom we find celebrated by the poets of that age, had assemblies at their houses, where persons of the best understanding, and of both sexes, met to pass the evenings in discoursing upon whatever agreeable subjects were occasionally started; and although we are apt to ridicule the sublime platonic notions they had, or personated, in love and friendship, I conceive their refinements were grounded upon reason, and that a little grain of the romance is no ill ingredient to preserve and exalt the dignity of human nature, without which it is apt to degenerate into everything that is sordid, vicious, and low. If there were no other use in the conversation of ladies, it is sufficient that it would lay a restraint upon those odious topics of immodesty and indecencies into which the rudeness of our northern genius is so apt to fall. And, therefore, it is observable in those sprightly gentlemen about the town who are so very dexterous at entertaining a vizard mask in the park or the playhouse, that in the company of ladies of virtue and honour, they are silent and disconcerted, and out of their element.

There are some people who think they sufficiently acquit themselves, and entertain their company with relating facts of no consequence, nor at all out of the road of such common incidents as happen every day; and this I have observed more frequently among the Scots than any other nation, who are very careful not to omit the minutest circumstances of time or place; which kind of discourse, if it were not a little relieved by the uncouth terms and phrases, as well as accent and gesture, peculiar to that country, would be hardly tolerable. It is not a fault in company to talk much, but to continue it long is certainly one; for if the majority of those who are got together be naturally silent or cautious, the conversation will flag unless it be often renewed by one among them who can start new subjects, provided he does not dwell upon them, that leave room for answers and replies.

I AM ONE OF THE SICKLY TRIBE . . .
(THE SPECTATOR, NO. 25)

Joseph Addison

Joseph Addison (1672–1719), essayist, poet, and playwright, is best remembered for the essays which he and Richard Steele wrote for their magazines, The Spectator and The Tatler. The Spectator, from which the following essay is taken, appeared six times a week for almost two years (1711–12). The majority of these papers were written by Addison. In addition to his renown as an essayist, he was also famous in his own time for having written one of the century's most successful plays, Cato (1713).

Dr. Samuel Johnson, speaking of Addison's style, called it "the model of the middle style; on grave subjects not formal, on light occasions not groveling; pure without scrupulosity, and exact without apparent elaboration; always equable, and always easy, without glowing words or pointed sentences." Although neither Addison nor Steele had the caustic pen of Jonathan Swift, their essays were generally used for similar criticism of the times. As wits and satirists, they exercised a kindly but steady pressure toward humanitarian reform.

Thursday, March 29, 1711

The following Letter will explain itself, and needs no Apology.

'Sir,

I am one of that sickly Tribe who are commonly known by the name of Valetudinarians;[1] and do confess to you, that I first contracted this ill Habit of Body, or rather of Mind, by the Study of Physick.[2] I no sooner began to peruse Books of this Nature, but I found my Pulse was irregular, and scarce

---

[1] *Valetudinarians:* weak or sickly persons who are overly preoccupied with their afflictions.
[2] *Physick:* medical science.

35

ever read the Account of any Disease that I did not fancy my self afflicted with. Doctor *Sydenham's* learned Treatise of Fevers threw me into a lingering Hectick, which hung upon me all the while I was reading that excellent Piece. I then applied my self to the Study of several Authors, who have written upon Phthisical Distempers,[3] and by that means fell into a Consumption; till at length, growing very fat, I was in a manner shamed out of that Imagination. Not long after this I found in my self all the Symptoms of the Gout, except Pain; but was cured of it by a Treatise upon the Gravel, written by a very Ingenious Author, who (as it is usual for Physicians to convert one Distemper into another) eased me out of the Gout by giving me the Stone. I at length studied my self into a Complication of Distempers; but, accidentally taking into my Hand that Ingenious Discourse written by *Sanctorius*, I was resolved to direct my self by a Scheme of Rules, which I had collected from his Observations. The Learned World are very well acquainted with that Gentleman's Invention; who, for the better carrying on of his Experiments, contrived a certain Mathematical Chair, which was so Artificially hung upon Springs, that it would weigh any thing as well as a Pair of Scales. By this means he discovered how many Ounces of his Food pass'd by Perspiration, what quantity of it was turned into Nourishment, and how much went away by the other Channels and Distributions of Nature.

Having provided my self with this Chair, I used to Study, Eat, Drink, and Sleep in it; insomuch that I may be said, for these three last Years, to have lived in a Pair of Scales. I compute my self, when I am in full Health, to be precisely Two hundred Weight, falling short of it about a Pound after a Day's Fast, and exceeding it as much after a very full Meal; so that it is my continual Employment to trim the Ballance between these two Volatile Pounds in my Constitution. In my ordinary Meals I fetch my self up to Two hundred Weight

[3] This and similar terms in the essay are now obsolete medical expressions.

and a half Pound; and if after having dined I find myself fall short of it, I drink just so much Small Beer, or eat such a quantity of Bread, as is sufficient to make me weight. In my greatest Excesses I do not transgress more than the other half Pound; which, for my Health's sake, I do the first *Monday* in every Month. As soon as I find my self duly poised after Dinner, I walk till I have perspired five Ounces and four Scruples; and when I discover, by my Chair, that I am so far reduced, I fall to my Books, and study away three Ounces more. As for the remaining Parts of the Pound, I keep no accompt of them. I do not dine and sup by the Clock, but by my Chair; for when that informs me my Pound of Food is exhausted I conclude my self to be hungry, and lay in another with all Diligence. In my Days of Abstinence I lose a Pound and an half, and on solemn Fasts am two Pound lighter than on other Days in the Year.

I allow my self, one Night with another, a Quarter of a Pound of Sleep within a few Grains more or less; and if upon my rising I find that I have not consumed my whole quantity, I take out the rest in my Chair. Upon an exact Calculation of what I expended and received the last Year, which I always register in a Book, I find the Medium to be Two hundred Weight, so that I cannot discover that I am impaired one Ounce in my Health during a whole Twelve-month. And yet, Sir, notwithstanding this my great Care to ballast my self equally every Day, and to keep my Body in its proper Poise, so it is that I find my self in a sick and languishing Condition. My Complexion is grown very sallow, my Pulse low, and my Body Hydropical. Let me therefore beg you, Sir, to consider me as your Patient, and to give me more certain Rules to walk by than those I have already observed, and you will very much oblige

Your Humble Servant.'

This letter puts me in mind of an *Italian* Epitaph written on the Monument of a Valetudinarian: *Stavo ben, mi per star*

meglio, sto qui: Which it is impossible to translate.[4] The Fear
of Death often proves Mortal, and sets People on Methods to
save their Lives, which infallibly destroy them. This is a reflection made by some Historians, upon observing that there are
many more thousands killed in a Flight than in a Battel; and
may be applied to those Multitudes of Imaginary Sick Persons
that break their Constitutions by Physick, and throw themselves into the Arms of Death, by endeavoring to escape it.
This Method is not only dangerous, but below the practice of a
Reasonable Creature. To consult the Preservation of Life, as
the only End of it, To make our Health our Business, To
engage in no Action that is not part of a Regimen, or course
of Physick; are Purposes so abject, so mean, so unworthy
human Nature, that a generous Soul would rather die than
submit to them. Besides, that a continual Anxiety for Life
vitiates all the Relishes of it, and casts a Gloom over the whole
Face of Nature; as it is impossible we should take Delight in
any thing that we are every Moment afraid of losing.

I do not mean, by what I have here said, that I think any one
to blame for taking due Care of their Health. On the contrary,
as Cheerfulness of Mind, and Capacity for Business, are in a
great measure the Effects of a well-tempered Constitution, a
Man cannot be at too much Pains to cultivate and preserve it.
But this Care, which we are prompted to, not only by common
Sense, but by Duty and Instinct, should never engage us in
groundless Fears, melancholy Apprehensions, and Imaginary
Distempers, which are natural to every Man who is more anxious
to live than how to live. In short, the Preservation of Life
should be only a secondary Concern, and the Direction of it
our Principal. If we have this Frame of Mind, we shall take
the best Means to preserve Life, without being over-solicitous
about the Event; and shall arrive at that Point of Felicity which

[4] "I was once well, but in order to become better [by medicines, study
of symptoms] I am here" [in the grave]. To paraphrase: "If I'd stayed
away from medicine, I'd be alive now!"

Martial[5] has mentioned as the Perfection of Happiness, of neither fearing nor wishing for Death.

In answer to the Gentleman, who tempers his Health by Ounces and by Scruples, and instead of complying with those natural Sollicitations of Hunger and Thirst, Drowsiness or Love of Exercise, governs himself by the Prescriptions of his Chair, I shall tell him a short Fable. *Jupiter*, says the Mythologist, to reward the Piety of a certain Countryman, promised to give him whatever he would ask. The Countryman desired that he might have the Management of the Weather in his own Estate: He obtained his Request, and immediately distributed Rain, Snow, and Sunshine among his several Fields, as he thought the nature of the Soil required. At the end of the Year, when he expected to see a more than ordinary Crop, his Harvest fell infinitely short of that of his Neighbours: Upon which (says the Fable) he desired *Jupiter* to take the Weather again into his own Hands, or that otherwise he should utterly ruin himself.

[5] Martial (first century A.D.) was a Roman writer of epigrams.

ON THE FEELING OF IMMORTALITY
IN YOUTH

William Hazlitt

William Hazlitt (1778–1830), English critic and essayist, was destined by his father for the Unitarian ministry, but he himself chose to go the way of art. For ten years he tried painting, but his interest in it slowly diminished; and after meeting Coleridge and Wordsworth, he turned to literature.

Hazlitt wrote primarily for magazines. Numerous as his essays are, each one seems fresh and original. He once remarked that he hated "anything that occupies more space than is worthy," and he applied this maxim to his own writing. His style is compact and deceptively simple, his approach is frequently impressionistic, revealing his sensitive nature, and his attitude is rational. As Hardin Craig suggested, "he taught himself to think, and this is the key to Hazlitt."

"Life is a pure flame, and we live by an invisible sun within us."
—Sir Thomas Browne, Urn Burial

No young man believes he shall ever die. It was a saying of my brother's, and a fine one. There is a feeling of Eternity in youth, which makes us amends for everything. To be young is to be as one of the Immortal Gods. One half of time indeed is flown—the other half remains in store for us with all its countless treasures; for there is no line drawn, and we see no limit to our hopes and wishes. We make the coming age our own.—

The vast, the unbounded prospect lies before us.

[From The Monthly Magazine, March, 1827.]

Death, old age, are words without a meaning, that pass by us like the idle air which we regard not. Others may have undergone, or may still be liable to them—we "bear a charmed life," which laughs to scorn all such sickly fancies. As in setting out on a delightful journey, we strain our eager gaze forward—

Bidding the lovely scenes at distance hail,—

and see no end to the landscape, new objects presenting themselves as we advance; so, in the commencement of life, we set no bounds to our inclinations, nor to the unrestricted opportunities of gratifying them. We have as yet found no obstacle, no disposition to flag; and it seems that we can go on so for ever. We look round in a new world, full of life, and motion, and ceaseless progress; and feel in ourselves all the vigour and spirit to keep pace with it, and do not foresee from any present symptoms how we shall be left behind in the natural course of things, decline into old age, and drop into the grave. It is the simplicity, and as it were *abstractedness* of our feelings in youth, that (so to speak) identifies us with nature, and (our experience being slight and our passions strong) deludes us into a belief of being immortal like it. Our short-lived connection with existence, we fondly flatter ourselves, is an indissoluble and lasting union—a honey-moon that knows neither coldness, jar, nor separation. As infants smile and sleep, we are rocked in the cradle of our wayward fancies, and lulled into security by the roar of the universe around us—we quaff the cup of life with eager haste without draining it, instead of which it only overflows the more—objects press around us, filling the mind with their magnitude and with the throng of desires that wait upon them, so that we have no room for the thoughts of death. From that plenitude of our being, we cannot change all at once to dust and ashes, we cannot imagine "this sensible, warm motion, to become a kneaded clod"—we are too much dazzled by the brightness of the waking dream around us to look into the darkness of the tomb. We no more see our end than our beginning: the one is lost in oblivion and vacancy, as the other is hid from us by the crowd and hurry of approaching events.

Or the grim shadow is seen lingering in the horizon, which we are doomed never to overtake, or whose last, faint, glimmering outline touches upon Heaven and translates us to the skies! Nor would the hold that life has taken of us permit us to detach our thoughts from present objects and pursuits, even if we would. What is there more opposed to health, than sickness; to strength and beauty, than decay and dissolution; to the active search of knowledge than mere oblivion? Or is there none of the usual advantage to bar the approach of Death, and mock his idle threats; Hope supplies their place, and draws a veil over the abrupt termination of all our cherished schemes. While the spirit of youth remains unimpaired, ere the "wine of life is drank up" we are like people intoxicated or in a fever, who are hurried away by the violence of their own sensations: it is only as present objects begin to pall upon the sense, as we have been disappointed in our favourite pursuits, cut off from our closest ties, that passion loosens its hold upon the breast, that we by degrees become weaned from the world, and allow ourselves to contemplate, "as in a glass, darkly," the possibility of parting with it for good. The example of others, the voice of experience, has no effect upon us whatever. Casualties we must avoid: the slow and deliberate advances of age we can play at *hide-and-seek* with. We think ourselves too lusty and too nimble for that blear-eyed decrepit old gentleman to catch us. Like the foolish fat scullion, in Sterne, when she hears that Master Bobby is dead, our only reflection is—"So am not I!" The idea of death, instead of staggering our confidence, rather seems to strengthen and enhance our possession and our enjoyment of life. Others may fall around us like leaves, or be mowed down like flowers by the scythe of Time: these are but tropes and figures to the unreflecting ears and overweening presumption of youth. It is not till we see the flowers of Love, Hope, and Joy, withering around us, and our own pleasures cut up by the roots, that we bring the moral home to ourselves, that we abate something of the wanton extravagance of our pretensions, or that the emptiness and dreariness of the prospect before us reconciles us to the stillness of the grave!

> Life! thou strange thing, that hast a power to feel
> Thou art, and to perceive that others are.

Well might the poet begin his indignant invective against an art, whose professed object is its destruction, with this animated apostrophe to life. Life is indeed a strange gift, and its privileges are most miraculous. Nor is it singular that when the splendid boon is first granted us, our gratitude, our admiration, and our delight should prevent us from reflecting on our own nothingness, or from thinking it will ever be recalled. Our first and strongest impressions are taken from the mighty scene that is opened to us, and we very innocently transfer its durability as well as magnificence to ourselves. So newly found, we cannot make up our minds to parting with it yet and at least put off that consideration to an indefinite term. Like a clown at a fair, we are full of amazement and rapture, and have no thoughts of going home, or that it will soon be night. We know our existence only from external objects, and we measure it by them. We can never be satisfied with gazing; and nature will still want us to look on and applaud. Otherwise, the sumptuous entertainment, "the feast of reason and the flow of soul," to which they were invited seems little better than a mockery and a cruel insult. We do not go from a play till the scene is ended, and the lights are ready to be extinguished. But the fair face of things still shines on; shall we be called away before the curtain falls, or ere we have scarce had a glimpse of what is going on? Like children, our step-mother Nature holds us up to see the raree-show of the universe; and then, as if life were a burthen to support, lets us instantly down again. Yet in that short interval, what "brave sublunary things" does not the spectacle unfold; like a bubble, at one minute reflecting the universe, and the next, shook to air!—To see the golden sun and the azure sky, the outstretched ocean, to walk upon the green earth, and to be lord of a thousand creatures, to look down giddy precipices or over distant flowery vales, to see the world spread out under one's finger in a map, to bring the stars near, to view the smallest insects in a microscope, to read history, and witness the revolutions of empires and the succession of generations, to hear of the glory of Sidon and Tyre, or Babylon and Susa, as of a faded pageant, and to say all these were, and are now nothing, to think that we exist in such a point of time, and in such a corner of space, to be at once spectators and a part of the moving scene, to watch the return of the seasons, of spring and autumn, to hear

—The stockdove plain amid the forest deep,
That drowsy rustles to the sighing gale—

to traverse desert wildernesses, to listen to the midnight choir, to visit lighted halls, or plunge into the dungeon's gloom, or sit in crowded theatres and see life itself mocked, to feel heat and cold, pleasure and pain, right and wrong, truth and falsehood, to study the works of art and refine the sense of beauty to agony, to worship fame and to dream of immortality, to have read Shakespeare and belong to the same species as Sir Isaac Newton; to be and to do all this, and then in a moment to be nothing, to have it all snatched from one like a juggler's ball or a phantasmagoria; there is something revolting and incredible to sense in the transition, and no wonder that, aided by youth and warm blood, and the flush of enthusiasm, the mind contrives for a long time to reject it with disdain and loathing as a monstrous and improbable fiction, like a monkey on a house-top, that is loath, amidst its fine discoveries and specious antics, to be tumbled head-long into the street, and crushed to atoms, the sport and laughter of the multitude!

The change, from the commencement to the close of life, appears like a fable, after it has taken place; how should we treat it otherwise than as a chimera before it has come to pass? There are some things that happen so long ago, places or persons we have formerly seen, of which such dim traces remain, we hardly know whether it was sleeping or waking they occurred; they are like dreams within the dream of life, a mist,

a film before the eye of memory, which, as we try to recall
them more distinctly, elude our notice altogether. It is but
natural that the lone interval that we thus look back upon,
should have appeared long and endless in prospect. There are
others so distinct and fresh, they seem but of yesterday—their
very vividness might be deemed a pledge of their permanence.
Then, however far back our impressions may go, we find others
still older (for our years are multiplied in youth); descriptions
of scenes that we had read, and people before our time, Priam
and the Trojan war; and even then, Nestor was old and dwelt
delighted on his youth, and spoke of the race of heroes that
were no more;—what wonder that, seeing this long line of
being pictured in our minds, and reviving as it were in us, we
should give ourselves involuntary credit for an indeterminate
period of existence? In the Cathedral at Peterborough there is
a monument to Mary, Queen of Scots, at which I used to gaze
when a boy, while the events of the period, all that had happened since, passed in review before me. If all this mass of
feeling and imagination could be crowded into a moment's
compass, what might not the whole of life be supposed to
contain? We are heirs of the past; we count upon the future as
our natural reversion. Besides, there are some of our early
impressions so exquisitely tempered, it appears that they must
always last—nothing can add to or take away from their sweetness and purity—the first breath of spring, the hyacinth dipped
in the dew, the mild lustre of the evening-star, the rainbow
after a storm—while we have the full enjoyment of these, we
must be young; and what can ever alter us in this respect?
Truth, friendship, love, books, are also proof against the canker
of time; and while we live but for them, we can never grow
old. We take out a new lease of existence from the objects on
which we set our affections, and become abstracted, impassive,
immortal in them. We cannot conceive how certain sentiments
should ever decay or grow cold in our breasts; and, consequently,
to maintain them in their first youthful glow and vigour, the
flame of life must continue to burn as bright as ever, or rather,
they are the fuel that feed the sacred lamp, that kindle "the

purple light of love," and spread a golden cloud around our
heads! Again, we not only flourish and survive in our affections
(in which we will not listen to the possibility of a change, any
more than we foresee the wrinkles on the brow of a mistress),
but we have a farther guarantee against the thoughts of death
in our favourite studies and pursuits, and in their continual
advance. Art we know is long; life, we feel, should be so too.
We see no end of the difficulties we have to encounter: perfection is slow of attainment, and we must have time to accomplish it in. Rubens complained that when he had just learnt
his art, he was snatched away from it: we trust we shall be more
fortunate! A wrinkle in an old head takes whole days to finish
it properly: but to catch "the Raphael grace, the Guido air,"
no limit should be put to our endeavours. What a prospect for
the future! What a task we have entered upon; and shall we
be arrested in the middle of it? We do not reckon our time
thus employed lost, or our pains thrown away, or our progress
slow—we do not droop or grow tired, but "gain new vigour
at our endless task";—and shall Time grudge us the opportunity to finish what we have auspiciously begun, and have
formed a sort of compact with nature to achieve? The fame
of the great names we look up to is also imperishable; and
shall not we, who contemplate it with such intense yearnings,
imbibe a portion of ethereal fire, the *divinae particula aurae*,[1]
which nothing can extinguish? I remember to have looked at a
print of Rembrandt for hours together, without being conscious of the flight of time, trying to resolve it into its com-
ponent parts, to connect its strong and sharp gradations, to
learn the secret of its reflected lights, and found neither satiety
nor pause in the prosecution of my studies. The print over
which I was poring would last long enough; why should the
idea in my mind, which was finer, more impalpable, perish
before it? At this, I redoubled the ardour of my pursuit, and
by the very subtlety and refinement of my inquiries, seemed to

[1] The immortal and divine breath or spirit. Greatness in man or his art
is infused, it is suggested, by this non-material essence.

bespeak for them an exemption from corruption and the rude grasp of Death.

Objects, on our first acquaintance with them, have that singleness and integrity of impression that it seems as if nothing could destroy or obliterate them, so firmly are they stamped and rivetted on the brain. We repose on them with a sort of voluptuous indolence, in full faith and boundless confidence. We are absorbed in the present moment, or return to the same point—idling away a great deal of time in youth, thinking we have enough and to spare. There is often a local feeling in the air, which is as fixed as if it were of marble; we loiter in dim cloisters, losing ourselves in thought and in their glimmering arches; a winding road before us seems as long as the journey of life, and as full of events. Time and experience dissipate this illusion; and by reducing them to detail, circumscribe the limits of our expectations. It is only as the pageant of life passes by and the masques turn their backs upon us, that we see through the deception, or believe that the train will have an end. In many cases, the slow progress and monotonous texture of our lives, before we mingle with the world and are embroiled in its affairs, has a tendency to aid the same feeling. We have a difficulty, when left to ourselves, and without the resource of books or some more lively pursuit, to "beguile the slow and creeping hours of time," and argue that if it moves on always at this tedious snail's-pace, it can never come to an end. We are willing to skip over certain portions of it that separate us from favourite objects, that irritate ourselves at the unnecessary delay. The young are prodigal of life from a superabundance of it; the old are tenacious on the same score, because they have little left, and cannot enjoy even what remains of it.

For my part, I set out in life with the French Revolution, and that event had considerable influence on my early feelings, as on those of others. Youth was then doubly such. It was the dawn of a new era, a new impulse had been given to men's minds, and the sun of Liberty rose upon the sun of Life in the same day, and both were proud to run their race together.

Little did I dream, while my first hopes and wishes went hand in hand with those of the human race, that long before my eyes should close, that dawn would be overcast, and set once more in the night of despotism—"total eclipse!" Happy that I did not. I felt for years, and during the best part of my existence, *heart-whole* in that cause, and triumphed in the triumphs over the enemies of man! At that time, while the fairest aspirations of the human mind seemed about to be realized, ere the image of man was defaced and his breast mangled in scorn, philosophy took a higher, poetry could afford a deeper range. At that time, to read the *Robbers*, was indeed delicious, and to hear

> From the dungeon of the tower time-rent,
> That fearful voice, a famish'd father's cry,

could be borne only amidst the fulness of hope, the crash of the fall of the strongholds of power, and the exulting sounds of the march of human freedom. What feelings the death-scene in *Don Carlos* sent into the soul! In that headlong career of lofty enthusiasm, and the joyous opening of the prospects of the world and our own, the thought of death crossing it smote doubly cold upon the mind; there was a stifling sense of oppression and confinement, an impatience of our present knowledge, a desire to grasp the whole of our existence in one strong embrace, to sound the mystery of life and death, and in order to put an end to the agony of doubt and dread, to burst through our prisonhouse, and confront the King of Terrors in his grisly palace! . . . As I was writing out this passage, my miniature-picture when a child lay on the mantel-piece, and I took it out of the case to look at it. I could perceive few traces of myself in it; but there was the same placid brow, the dimpled mouth, the same timid, inquisitive glance as ever. But its careless smile did not seem to reproach me with having become a recreant to the sentiments that were then sown in my mind, or with having written a sentence that could call up a blush in this image of ingenuous youth!

"That time is past with all its giddy raptures." Since the

future was barred to my progress, I have turned for consolation
to the past, gathering up the fragments of my early recollections,
and putting them into a form that might live. It is thus, that
when we find our personal and substantial identity vanishing
from us, we strive to gain a reflected and substituted one in our
thoughts: we do not like to perish wholly, and wish to bequeath
our names at least to posterity. As long as we can keep alive
our cherished thoughts and nearest interests in the minds of
others, we do not appear to have retired altogether from the
stage, we still occupy a place in the estimation of mankind,
exercise a powerful influence over them, and it is only our
bodies that are trampled into dust or dispersed to air. Our
darling speculations still find favour and encouragement, and
we make as good a figure in the eyes of our descendants, nay,
perhaps, a better than we did in our life-time. This is one
point gained; the demands of our self-love are so far satisfied.
Besides, if by the proofs of intellectual superiority we survive
ourselves in this world, by exemplary virtue or unblemished
faith we are taught to ensure an interest in another and a
higher state of being, and to anticipate at the same time the
applauses of men and angels.

> Even from the tomb the voice of nature cries;
> Even in our ashes live their wonted fires.

As we advance in life, we acquire a keener sense of the value
of time. Nothing else, indeed, seems of any consequence; and
we become misers in this respect. We try to arrest its few last
tottering steps, and to make it linger on the brink of the grave.
We can never leave off wondering how that which has ever
been should cease to be, and would still live on, that we may
wonder at our own shadow, and when "all the life of life is
flown," dwell on the retrospect of the past. This is accompanied
by a mechanical tenaciousness of whatever we possess, by a
distrust and a sense of fallacious hollowness in all we see.
Instead of the full, pulpy feeling of youth, everything is flat
and insipid. The world is a painted witch, that puts us off with
false shows and tempting appearances. The ease, the jocund

gaiety, the unsuspecting security of youth are fled: nor can we, without flying in the face of common sense,

> From the last dregs of life, hope to receive
> What its first sprightly runnings could not give.

If we can slip out of the world without notice or mischance, can tamper with bodily infirmity, and frame our minds to the becoming composure of *still-life*, before we sink into total insensibility, it is as much as we ought to expect. We do not in the regular course of nature die all at once: we have mouldered away gradually long before; faculty after faculty, attachment after attachment, we are torn from ourselves piecemeal while living; year after year takes something from us; and death only consigns the last remnant of what we were to the grave. The revulsion is not so great, and a quiet *euthanasia* is a winding-up of the plot, that is not out of reason or nature.

That we should thus in a manner outlive ourselves, and dwindle imperceptibly into nothing, is not surprising, when even in our prime the strongest impressions leave so little traces of themselves behind, and the last object is driven out by the succeeding one. How little effect is produced on us at any time by the books we have read, the scenes we have witnessed, the sufferings we have gone through! Think only of the variety of feelings we experience in reading an interesting romance, or being present at a fine play—what beauty, what sublimity, what soothing, what heart-rending emotions! You would suppose these would last for ever, or at least subdue the mind to a correspondent tone and harmony—while we turn over the page, while the scene is passing before us, it seems as if nothing could ever after shake our resolution, that "treason domestic, foreign levy, nothing could touch us farther!" The first splash of mud we get, on entering the street, the first pettifogging shop-keeper that cheats us out of twopence, and the whole vanishes clean out of our remembrance, and we become the idle prey of the most petty and annoying circumstances. The mind soars by an effort to the grand and lofty: it is at home in the grovelling, the disagreeable, and the little. This happens in the height and heyday of our existence, when novelty gives a stronger impulse to the blood and takes a faster hold of the brain, (I have known the impression on coming out of a gallery of pictures then last half a day)—as we grow old, we become more feeble and querulous, every object "reverbs its own hollowness," and both worlds are not enough to satisfy the peevish importunity and extravagant presumption of our desires! There are a few superior, happy beings, who are born with a temper exempt from every trifling annoyance. This spirit sits serene and smiling as in its native skies, and a divine harmony (whether heard or not) plays around them. This is to be at peace. Without this, it is in vain to fly into deserts, or to build a hermitage on the top of rocks, if regret and ill-humour follow us there: and with this, it is needless to make the experiment. The only true retirement is that of the heart; the only true leisure is the repose of the passions. To such persons it makes little difference whether they are young or old; and they die as they have lived, with graceful resignation.

OLD CHINA

Charles Lamb

Charles Lamb (1775–1834) turned from unsuccessful playwriting to the familiar essay. He was immediately succesful in the genre, and published numerous sketches, under the pseudonym Elia, in the leading magazines of his period. He was widely acclaimed, and today is one of the best-loved of informal essayists.

Though Lamb could invest the simplest, most ordinary object with such charm that it became unusual and quaint when he wrote of it, he obviously preferred as a subject that which was by its nature already unusual and quaint. In "Old China," he gives us a glimpse into the household he shared with Mary, his beloved sister, who was afflicted with insanity. "Old China" illustrates the discursive method often used by the informal essayist. Lamb's seemingly casual prose magically moves the essay from the particular to the general, to a serious discussion of certain values in human life which stand apart from wealth and easily acquired material possessions.

I have an almost feminine partiality for old china. When I go to see any great house, I inquire for the china-closet, and next for the picture-gallery. I cannot defend the order of preference but by saying that we have all some taste or other, of too ancient a date to admit of our remembering distinctly that it was an acquired one. I can call to mind the first play, and the first exhibition, that I was taken to; but I am not conscious of a time when china jars and saucers were introduced into my imagination.

I had no repugnance then—why should I now have?—to those little, lawless, azure-tinctured grotesques that, under the notion of men and women, float about, uncircumscribed by any element, in that world before perspective—a china teacup.

[*From The* Last Essays of Elia (1833).]

I like to see my old friends—whom distance cannot diminish —figuring up in the air (so they appear to our optics), yet on *terra firma* still—for so we must in courtesy interpret that speck of deeper blue, which the decorous artist, to prevent absurdity, had made to spring up beneath their sandals.

I love the men with women's faces, and the women, if possible, with still more womanish expressions.

Here is a young and courtly Mandarin, handing tea to a lady from a salver—two miles off. See how distance seems to set off respect! And here the same lady, or another—for likeness is identity on teacups—is stepping into a little fairy boat, moored on the hither side of this calm garden river, with a dainty mincing foot, which in a right angle of incidence (as angles go in our world) must infallibly land her in the midst of a flowery mead—a furlong off on the other side of the same strange stream!

Farther on—if far or near can be predicated of their world— see horses, trees, pagodas, dancing the hays.

Here—a cow and rabbit couchant, and coextensive—so objects show, seen through the lucid atmosphere of fine Cathay.[1]

I was pointing out to my cousin last evening, over our Hyson (which we are old-fashioned enough to drink unmixed still of an afternoon), some of these *speciosa miracula*[2] upon a set of extraordinary old blue china (a recent purchase) which we were now for the first time using; and could not help remarking how favorable circumstances had been to us of late years, that we could afford to please the eye sometimes with trifles of this sort—when a passing sentiment seemed to overshade the brows of my companion. I am quick at detecting these summer clouds in Bridget.[3]

"I wish the good old times would come again," she said, "when we were not quite so rich. I do not mean that I want to be poor; but there was a middle state"—so she was pleased to ramble on—"in which I am sure we were a great deal happier.

[1] China.
[2] Fanciful scenes or pictures.
[3] Bridget was Lamb's sister, Mary.

A purchase is but a purchase, now that you have money enough and to spare. Formerly it used to be a triumph. When we coveted a cheap luxury (and O! how much ado I had to get you to consent in those times!)—we were used to have a debate two or three days before, and to weigh the *for* and *against*, and think what we might spare it out of, and what saving we could hit upon, that should be an equivalent. A thing was worth buying then, when we felt the money that we paid for it.

"Do you remember the brown suit which you made to hang upon you till all your friends cried shame upon you, it grew so threadbare—and all because of that folio Beaumont and Fletcher,[4] which you dragged home late at night from Barker's in Covent Garden? Do you remember how we eyed it for weeks before we could make up our minds to the purchase, and had not come to a determination till it was near ten o'clock of the Saturday night, when you set off from Islington, fearing you should be too late—and when the old bookseller with some grumbling opened his shop, and by the twinkling taper (for he was setting bedward) lighted out the relic from his dusty treasures—and when you lugged it home, wishing it were twice as cumbersome—and when you presented it to me —and when we were exploring the perfectness of it (*collating*, you called it)—and while I was repairing some of the loose leaves with paste, which your impatience would not suffer to be left till daybreak—was there no pleasure in being a poor man? Or can those neat black clothes which you wear now, and are so careful to keep brushed, since we have become rich and finical—give you half the honest vanity with which you flaunted it about in that overworn suit—your old corbeau—for four or five weeks longer than you should have done, to pacify your conscience for the mighty sum of fifteen—or sixteen shillings was it?—a great affair we thought it then—which you had lavished on the old folio. Now you can afford to buy any book that pleases you, but I do not see that you ever bring me home any nice old purchases now.

[4] Early seventeenth-century English dramatists who collaborated in the writing of many plays.

"When you came home with twenty apologies for laying out a less number of shillings upon that print after Lionardo,[5] which we christened the 'Lady Blanch'; when you looked at the purchase, and thought of the money—and thought of the money, and looked again at the picture—was there no pleasure in being a poor man? Now you have nothing to do but to walk into Colnaghi's, and buy a wilderness of Lionardos. Yet do you?

"Then, do you remember our pleasant walks to Enfield, and Potter's Bar, and Waltham, when we had a holiday—holidays and all other fun are gone now we are rich—and the little hand-basket in which I used to deposit our day's fare of savory cold lamb and salad—and how you would pry about at noontide for some decent house, where we might go in and produce our store—only paying for the ale that you must call for—and speculate upon the looks of the landlady, and whether she was likely to allow us a tablecloth—and wish for such another honest hostess as Izaak Walton[6] has described many a one on the pleasant banks of the Lea, when he went a-fishing—and sometimes they would prove obliging enough, and sometimes they would look grudgingly upon us—but we had cheerful looks still for one another, and would eat our plain food savorily, scarcely grudging Piscator[7] his Trout Hall? Now—when we go out a day's pleasuring, which is seldom, moreover, we *ride* part of the way, and go into a fine inn, and order the best of dinners, never debating the expense—which, after all, never has half the relish of those chance country snaps, when we were at the mercy of uncertain usage, and a precarious welcome.

"You are too proud to see a play anywhere now but in the pit. Do you remember where it was we used to sit, when we saw the *Battle of Hexham*, and the *Surrender of Calais*, and Bannister and Mrs. Bland in the *Children in the Wood*—when

---

[5] Leonardo da Vinci (1452–1519), the famous Florentine painter, sculptor, scientist, and engineer.

[6] Izaak Walton (1593–1683) was an English writer, the author of *The Compleat Angler*.

[7] *Piscator*: a character, a fisherman, in *The Compleat Angler*. Trout Hall was Piscator's favorite inn.

we squeezed out our shillings apiece to sit three or four times in a season in the one-shilling gallery—where you felt all the time that you ought not to have brought me—and more strongly I felt obligation to you for having brought me—and the pleasure was the better for a little shame—and when the curtain drew up, what cared we for our place in the house, or what mattered it where we were sitting, when our thoughts were with Rosalind in Arden,[8] or with Viola at the Court of Illyria? You used to say that the gallery was the best place of all for enjoying a play socially—that the relish of such exhibitions must be in proportion to the infrequency of going—that the company we met there, not being in general readers of plays, were obliged to attend the more, and did attend, to what was going on, on the stage—because a word lost would have been a chasm, which it was impossible for them to fill up. With such reflections we consoled our pride then—and I appeal to you whether, as a woman, I met generally with less attention and accommodation than I have done since in more expensive situations in the house? The getting in, indeed, and the crowding up those inconvenient staircases, was bad enough—but there was still a law of civility to women recognized to quite as great an extent as we ever found in the other passages—and how a little difficulty overcome heightened the snug seat and the play, afterwards! Now we can only pay our money and walk in. You cannot see, you say, in the galleries now. I am sure we saw, and heard, too, well enough then—but sight, and all, I think, is gone with our poverty.

"There was pleasure in eating strawberries, before they became quite common—in the first dish of peas, while they were yet dear—to have them for a nice supper, a treat. What treat can we have now? If we were to treat ourselves now—that is, to have dainties a little above our means, it would be selfish and wicked. It is the very little more that we allow ourselves beyond what the actual poor can get at that makes what I call a treat—when two people, living together as we have done, now and then indulge themselves in a cheap luxury,

[8] Characters in Shakespeare's *As You Like It* and *Twelfth Night*.

which both like; while each apologizes, and is willing to take both halves of the blame to his single share. I see no harm in people making much of themselves, in that sense of the word. It may give them a hint how to make much of others. But now —what I mean by the word—we never *do* make much of ourselves. None but the poor can do it. I do not mean the veriest poor of all, but persons as we were, just above poverty.

"I know what you were going to say, that it is mighty pleasant at the end of the year to make all meet—and much ado we used to have every thirty-first night of December to account for our exceedings—many a long face did you make over your puzzled accounts, and in contriving to make it out how we had spent so much—or that we had not spent so much—or that it was impossible we should spend so much next year—and still we found our slender capital decreasing—but then—betwixt ways, and projects, and compromises of one sort or another, and talk of curtailing this charge, and doing without that for the future—and the hope that youth brings, and laughing spirits (in which you were never poor till now), we pocketed up our loss, and in conclusion, with 'lusty brimmers' (as you used to quote it out of *hearty cheerful Mr. Cotton,*[9] as you called him), we used to welcome in the 'coming guest.' Now we have no reckoning at all at the end of the old year—no flattering promises about the new year doing better for us."

Bridget is so sparing of her speech on most occasions that when she gets into a rhetorical vein, I am careful how I interrupt it. I could not help, however, smiling at the phantom of wealth which her dear imagination had conjured up out of a clear income of poor —— hundred pounds a year. "It is true we were happier when we were poorer, but we were also younger, my cousin. I am afraid we must put up with the excess, for if we were to shake the superflux into the sea, we should not much mend ourselves. That we had much to struggle with, as we grew up together, we have reason to be most

[9] Charles Cotton (1630–1687), an English writer and translator who wrote, among many other things, a sequel to Walton's *The Compleat Angler*.

thankful. It strengthened and knit our compact closer. We could never have been what we have been to each other if we had always had the sufficiency which you now complain of. The resisting power—those natural dilations of the youthful spirit, which circumstances cannot straiten—with us are long since passed away. Competence to age is supplementary youth, a sorry supplement indeed, but I fear the best that is to be had. We must ride where we formerly walked; live better and lie softer—and shall be wise to do so—than we had means to do in those good old days you speak of. Yet could those days return—could you and I once more walk our thirty miles a day— could Bannister and Mrs. Bland again be young, and you and I be young to see them—could the good old one-shilling gallery days return—they are dreams, my cousin, now—but could you and I at this moment, instead of this quiet argument, by our well-carpeted fireside, sitting on this luxurious sofa—be once more struggling up those inconvenient staircases, pushed about and squeezed, and elbowed by the poorest rabble of poor gallery scramblers—could I once more hear those anxious shrieks of yours—and the delicious *Thank God, we are safe,* which always followed when the topmost stair, conquered, let in the first light of the whole cheerful theater down beneath us—I know not the fathom line that ever touched a descent so deep as I would be willing to bury more wealth in than Crœsus had, or the great Jew R—— is supposed to have, to purchase it. And now do just look at that merry little Chinese waiter holding an umbrella, big enough for a bed-tester, over the head of that pretty insipid half Madonna-ish chit of a lady in that very blue summer house." (1823)

SOLITUDE

Ralph Waldo Emerson

Ralph Waldo Emerson (1803–1882), *poet, essayist, and lecturer, was the leading figure in the American literary and philosophical movement known as Transcendentalism. A loosely-knit group at best, the Transcendentalists might most easily be identified by their admiration and respect for Emerson's short volume,* Nature, *published in 1836.*

"Solitude," the first chapter of the book, presents Emerson's philosophical concepts of the universe divided into nature and soul, of the ultimate harmony of man and nature, and of man's ability and necessity to transcend (hence the name Transcendentalist) material phenomena and become a part of the Oversoul.

To go into solitude, a man needs to retire as much from his chamber as from society. I am not solitary whilst I read and write, though nobody is with me. But if a man would be alone, let him look at the stars. The rays that come from those heavenly worlds will separate between him and what he touches. One might think the atmosphere was made transparent with this design, to give man, in the heavenly bodies, the perpetual presence of the sublime. Seen in the streets of cities, how great they are! If the stars should appear one night in a thousand years, how would men believe and adore; and preserve for many generations the remembrance of the city of God which had been shown! But every night come out these envoys of beauty, and light the universe with their admonishing smile.

The stars awaken a certain reverence, because though always present, they are inaccessible; but all natural objects make a kindred impression, when the mind is open to their influence. Nature never wears a mean appearance. Neither does the

[*From* Nature (1836).]

wisest man extort her secret, and lose his curiosity by finding out all her perfection. Nature never became a toy to a wise spirit. The flowers, the animals, the mountains, reflected the wisdom of his best hour, as much as they had delighted the simplicity of his childhood.

When we speak of nature in this manner, we have a distinct but most poetical sense in the mind. We mean the integrity of impression made by manifold natural objects. It is this which distinguishes the stick of timber of the wood-cutter from the tree of the poet. The charming landscape which I saw this morning is indubitably made up of some twenty or thirty farms. Miller owns this field, Locke that, and Manning the woodland beyond. But none of them owns the landscape. There is a property in the horizon which no man has but he whose eye can integrate all the parts, that is, the poet. This is the best part of these men's farms, yet to this their warranty-deeds give no title.

To speak truly, few adult persons can see nature. Most persons do not see the sun. At least they have a very superficial seeing. The sun illuminates only the eye of the man, but shines into the eye and the heart of the child. The lover of nature is he whose inward and outward senses are still truly adjusted to each other; who has retained the spirit of infancy even into the era of manhood. His intercourse with heaven and earth becomes part of his daily food. In the presence of nature a wild delight runs through the man, in spite of real sorrows. Nature says—he is my creature, and maugre all his impertinent griefs, he shall be glad with me. Not the sun or the summer alone, but every hour and season yields its tribute of delight; for every hour and change corresponds to and authorizes a different state of the mind, from breathless noon to grimmest midnight. Nature is a setting that fits equally well a comic or a mourning piece. In good health, the air is a cordial of incredible virtue. Crossing a bare common, in snow puddles, at twilight, under a clouded sky, without having in my thoughts any occurrence of special good fortune, I have enjoyed a perfect exhilaration. I am glad to the brink of fear. In the woods, too, a man casts off his years, as the snake his slough, and at what period soever of life is always a child. In the woods is perpetual youth. Within these plantations of God, a decorum and sanctity reign, a perennial festival is dressed, and the guest sees not how he should tire of them in a thousand years. In the woods, we return to reason and faith. There I feel that nothing can befall me in life—no disgrace, no calamity (leaving me my eyes), which nature cannot repair. Standing on the bare ground—my head bathed by the blithe air and uplifted into infinite space—all mean egotism vanishes. I become a transparent eyeball; I am nothing; I see all; the currents of the Universal Being circulate through me; I am part or parcel of God. The name of the nearest friend sounds then foreign and accidental: to be brothers, to be acquaintances, master or servant, is then a trifle and a disturbance. I am the lover of uncontained and immortal beauty. In the wilderness, I find something more dear and connate than in streets or villages. In the tranquil landscape, and especially in the distant line of the horizon, man beholds somewhat as beautiful as his own nature.

The greatest delight which the fields and woods minister is the suggestion of an occult relation between man and the vegetable. I am not alone and unacknowledged. They nod to me, and I to them. The waving of the boughs in the storm is new to me and old. It takes me by surprise, and yet is not unknown. Its effect is like that of a higher thought or a better emotion coming over me, when I deemed I was thinking justly or doing right.

Yet it is certain that the power to produce this delight does not reside in nature, but in man, or in a harmony of both. It is necessary to use these pleasures with great temperance. For nature is not always tricked in holiday attire, but the same scene which yesterday breathed perfume and glittered as for the frolic of the nymphs is overspread with melancholy to-day. Nature always wears the colors of the spirit. To a man laboring under calamity, the heat of his own fire hath sadness in it. Then there is a kind of contempt of the landscape felt by him who had just lost by death a dear friend. The sky is less grand as it shuts down over less worth in the population.

THE SHIP WRECK

Henry David Thoreau

Henry David Thoreau (1817–1862) has been called a "poet-naturalist," even though he wrote mostly in the essay form. In his essays he attempted to describe external phenomena naturalistically and then draw from these descriptions poetic and philosophic conclusions.

Cape Cod, from which "The Ship Wreck" is taken, is less well known than Thoreau's account of his life in the woods, Walden *(1854), but it shows equally well his concern with different aspects of nature, a concern which led him to the universal meanings embodied in material facts.*

Wishing to get a better view than I had yet had of the ocean, which, we are told, covers more than two thirds of the globe, but of which a man who lives a few miles inland may never see any trace, more than of another world, I made a visit to Cape Cod in October, 1849, another the succeeding June, and another to Truro in July, 1855; the first and last time with a single companion, the second time alone. I have spent, in all, about three weeks on the Cape; walked from Eastham to Provincetown twice on the Atlantic side, and once on the Bay side also, excepting four or five miles, and crossed the Cape half a dozen times on my way; but having come so fresh to the sea, I have got but little salted. My readers must expect only so much saltness as the land breeze acquires from blowing over an arm of the sea, or is tasted on the windows and the bark of trees twenty miles inland, after September gales. I have been accustomed to make excursions to the ponds within ten miles of Concord, but latterly I have extended my excursions to the seashore. . . .

We left Concord, Massachusetts, on Tuesday, October 9,

[*From* Cape Cod (*Norton, 1951*).]

1849. On reaching Boston, we found that the Provincetown
steamer, which should have got in the day before, had not yet
arrived, on account of a violent storm; and, as we noticed in the
streets a handbill headed, "Death! one hundred and forty-five
lives lost at Cohasset," we decided to go by way of Cohasset.
We found many Irish in the cars, going to identify bodies and
to sympathize with the survivors, and also to attend the funeral
which was to take place in the afternoon; and when we arrived
at Cohasset, it appeared that nearly all the passengers were
bound for the beach, which was about a mile distant, and many
other persons were flocking in from the neighboring country.
There were several hundreds of them streaming off over Cohasset common in that direction, some on foot and some in wagons,—and among them were some sportsmen in their hunting-
jackets, with their guns, and game-bags, and dogs. As we
passed the graveyard we saw a large hole, like a cellar, freshly
dug there, and, just before reaching the shore, by a pleas-
antly winding and rocky road, we met several hay-riggings and
farm-wagons coming away toward the meeting-house, each
loaded with three large, rough deal boxes. We did not need to
ask what was in them. The owners of the wagons were made
the undertakers. Many horses in carriages were fastened to the
fences near the shore, and, for a mile or more, up and down, the
beach was covered with people looking out for bodies, and examining the fragments of the wreck. There was a small island
called Brook Island, with a hut on it, lying just off the shore.
This is said to be the rockiest shore in Massachusetts, from
Nantasket to Scituate,—hard sienitic rocks,[1] which the waves
have laid bare, but have not been able to crumble. It has been
the scene of many a shipwreck.

The brig St. John, from Galway, Ireland, laden with emi-
grants, was wrecked on Sunday morning; it was now Tuesday
morning, and the sea was still breaking violently on the rocks.
There were eighteen or twenty of the same large boxes that I
have mentioned, lying on a green hillside, a few rods from the
water, and surrounded by a crowd. The bodies which had been

[1] Granite.

recovered, twenty-seven or eight in all, had been collected there. Some were rapidly nailing down the lids; others were carting the boxes away; and others were lifting the lids, which were yet loose, and peeping under the cloths, for each body, with such rags as still adhered to it, was covered loosely with a white sheet. I witnessed no signs of grief, but there was a sober dispatch of business which was affecting. One man was seeking to identify a particular body, and one undertaker or carpenter was calling to another to know in what box a certain child was put. I saw many marble feet and matted heads as the cloths were raised, and one livid, swollen, and mangled body of a drowned girl,—who probably had intended to go out to service in some American family,—to which some rags still adhered, with a string, half concealed by the flesh, about its swollen neck; the coiled-up wreck of a human hulk, gashed by the rocks or fishes, so that the bone and muscle were exposed, but quite bloodless,—merely red and white,—with wide-open and staring eyes, yet lusterless, dead-lights; or like the cabin windows of a stranded vessel, filled with sand. Sometimes there were two or more children, or a parent and child, in the same box, and on the lid would perhaps be written with red chalk, "Bridget such-a-one, and sister's child." The surrounding sward was covered with bits of sails and clothing. I have since heard, from one who lives by this beach, that a woman who had come over before, but had left her infant behind for her sister to bring, came and looked into these boxes, and saw in one—probably the same whose superscription I have quoted—her child in her sister's arms, as if the sister had meant to be found thus; and, within three days after, the mother died from the effect of that sight.

We turned from this and walked along the rocky shore. In the first cove were strewn what seemed the fragments of a vessel, in small pieces mixed with sand and seaweed, and great quantities of feathers; but it looked so old and rusty, that I at first took it to be some old wreck which had lain there many years. I even thought of Captain Kidd, and that the feathers were those which sea-fowl had cast there; and perhaps there might be some tradition about it in the neighbourhood. I asked a sailor if that was the St. John. He said it was. I asked him where she struck. He pointed to a rock in front of us, a mile from the shore, called the Grampus Rock, and added,—

"You can see a great part of her now sticking up; it looks like a small boat."

I saw it. It was thought to be held by the chain-cables and the anchors. I asked if the bodies which I saw were all that were drowned.

"Not a quarter of them," said he.

"Where are the rest?"

"Most of them right underneath that piece you see."

It appeared to us that there was enough rubbish to make the wreck of a large vessel in this cove alone, and that it would take many days to cart it off. It was several feet deep, and here and there was a bonnet or a jacket on it. In the very midst of the crowd about this wreck there were men with carts busily collecting the seaweed which the storm had cast up, and conveying it beyond the reach of the tide, though they were often obliged to separate fragments of clothing from it, and they might at any moment have found a human body under it. Drown who might, they did not forget that this weed was a valuable manure. This shipwreck had not produced a visible vibration in the fabric of society.

About a mile south we could see, rising above the rocks, the masts of the British brig which the St. John had endeavored to follow, which had slipped her cables, and, by good luck, run into the mouth of Cohasset harbor. A little further along the shore we saw a man's clothes on a rock; further, a woman's scarf, a gown, a straw bonnet, the brig's caboose, and one of her masts high and dry, broken into several pieces. In another rocky cove, several rods from the water, and behind rocks twenty feet high, lay a part of one side of the vessel, still hanging together. It was, perhaps, forty feet long by fourteen wide. I was even more surprised at the power of the waves, exhibited on this shattered fragment, than I had been at the sight of the smaller fragments before. The largest timbers and iron braces were broken superfluously, and I saw that no material could withstand the power of the waves; that iron must go to pieces in such a case, and an iron vessel would be cracked up like an egg-shell on the rocks. Some of these timbers, however, were so rotten that I could almost thrust my umbrella through them. They told us that some were saved on this piece, and also showed where the sea had heaved it into this cove which was now dry. When I saw where it had come in, and in what condition, I wondered that any had been saved on it. A little further on, a crowd of men was collected around the mate of the St. John, who was telling his story. He was a slim-looking youth, who spoke of the captain as the master, and seemed a little excited. He was saying that when they jumped into the boat she filled, and, the vessel lurching, the weight of the water in the boat caused the painter to break, and so they were separated. Whereat one man came away saying,—

"Well, I don't see but he tells a straight story enough. You see, the weight of the water in the boat broke the painter. A boat full of water is very heavy,"—and so on, in a loud and impertinently earnest tone, as if he had a bet depending on it, but had no humane interest in the matter.

Another, a large man, stood near by upon a rock, gazing into the sea, and chewing large quids of tobacco, as if that habit were forever confirmed with him.

"Come," says another to his companion, "let's be off. We've seen the whole of it. It's no use to stay to the funeral."

Further, we saw one standing upon a rock who, we were told, was one that was saved. He was a sober-looking man, dressed in a jacket and gray pantaloons, with his hands in the pockets. I asked him a few questions, which he answered; but he seemed unwilling to talk about it, and soon walked away. By his side stood one of the lifeboat men, in an oil-cloth jacket, who told us how they went to the relief of the British brig, thinking that the boat of the St. John, which they passed on the way, held all her crew,—for the waves prevented their seeing those who were on the vessel, though they might have saved some had they known there were any there. A little further was the flag of the St. John, spread on a rock to dry, and held down by stones at the corners. This frail but essential and significant portion of the vessel, which had so long been the sport of the winds, was sure to reach the shore. There were one or two houses visible from these rocks, in which were some of the survivors recovering from the shock which their bodies and minds had sustained. One was not expected to live.

We kept on down the shore as far as a promontory called Whitehead, that we might see more of the Cohasset Rocks. In a little cove, within half a mile, there were an old man and his son collecting, with their team, the seaweed which that fatal storm had cast up, as serenely employed as if there had never been a wreck in the world, though they were within sight of the Grampus Rock, on which the St. John had struck. The old man had heard that there was a wreck and knew most of the particulars, but he said that he had not been up there since it happened. It was the wrecked weed that concerned him most, —rock-weed, kelp, and seaweed, as he named them,—which he carted to his barnyard; and those bodies were to him but other weeds which the tide cast up, but which were of no use to him. We afterwards came to the lifeboat in its harbor, waiting for another emergency; and in the afternoon we saw the funeral procession at a distance, at the head of which walked the captain with the other survivors.

On the whole, it was not so impressive a scene as I might have expected. If I had found one body cast upon the beach in some lonely place, it would have affected me more. I sympathized rather with the winds and waves, as if to toss and mangle these poor human bodies was the order of the day. If this was the law of Nature, why waste any time in awe or pity? If the last day were come, we should not think so much about the separation of friends or the blighted prospects of individuals. I saw that corpses might be multiplied, as on the field of battle, till they no longer affected us in any degree, as exceptions to the common lot of humanity. Take all the graveyards together, they are always the majority. It is the individual and private that demands our sympathy. A man can attend but one funeral in the course of his life, can behold but one corpse. Yet I saw that the inhabitants of the shore would be not a little affected by this event. They would watch there many days and nights for the sea to give up its dead, and their imaginations and sympathies would supply the place of mourners far away, who as yet knew not of the wreck. Many days after this, something white was seen floating on the water by one who was sauntering on the beach. It was approached in a boat, and found to be the body of a woman, which had risen in an upright position, whose white cap was blown back with the wind. I saw that the beauty of the shore itself was wrecked for many a lonely walker there, until he could perceive, at last, how its beauty was enhanced by wrecks like this, and it acquired thus a rarer and sublimer beauty still.

Why care for these dead bodies? They really have no friends but the worms or fishes. Their owners were coming to the New World, as Columbus and the Pilgrims did,—they were within a mile of its shores; but, before they could reach it, they emigrated to a newer world than ever Columbus dreamed of, yet one of whose existence we believe that there is far more universal and convincing evidence—though it has not yet been discovered by science—than Columbus had of this: not merely mariner's tales and some paltry driftwood and seaweed, but a continual drift and instinct to all our shores. I saw their empty hulks that came to land; but they themselves, meanwhile, were cast upon some shore yet further west, toward which we are all tending, and which we shall reach at last, it may be through storm and darkness as they did. No doubt we have reason to thank God that they have not been "shipwrecked into life again." The mariner who makes the safest port in heaven, perchance, seems to his friends on earth to be shipwrecked, for they deem Boston harbor the better place: though perhaps invisible to them, a skillful pilot comes to meet him, and the fairest and balmiest gales blow off that coast, his good ship makes the land in halcyon days, and he kisses the shore in rapture there, while his old hulk tosses in the surf here. It is hard to part with one's body, but no doubt it is easy enough to do without it when once it is gone. All their plans and hopes burst like a bubble! Infants by the score dashed on the rocks by the enraged Atlantic Ocean! No, no! If the St. John did not make her port here, she has been telegraphed there. The strongest wind cannot stagger a spirit; it is a spirit's breath. A just man's purpose cannot be split on any Grampus or material rock, but itself will split rocks till it succeeds.

AURELIA'S UNFORTUNATE YOUNG MAN

Samuel L. Clemens

*Samuel Langhorne Clemens (1835–1910), better known as Mark
Twain, was an American humorist, novelist, essayist, and lecturer.
Printer's apprentice, newspaper writer, boat pilot, and traveler in
the western United States, he lived a full and, in his late years, a
tragic life. Beneath his informal and humorous writing, there must
have always been an awareness of the essential grimness of life.
"Aurelia's Unfortunate Young Man" illustrates how humor of the
wildest sort can be drawn from disastrous events, and thus it reveals
the paradoxical alliance between humor and suffering. In his more
disturbed moments, when his art was no longer adequate to his
feelings, Twain knew that "everything human is pathetic. The
secret source of humor is not joy but sorrow. There is no humor in
heaven."*

*This sketch is the sort of droll, extended relation of incredible
events, the sort of tall tale casually told, that distinguished Twain's
career as a popular lecturer.*

The facts in the following case came to me by letter from a
young lady who lives in the beautiful city of San José; she is
perfectly unknown to me, and simply signs herself "Aurelia
Maria," which may possibly be a fictitious name. But no matter, the poor girl is almost heart-broken by the misfortunes she
has undergone, and so confused by the conflicting counsels of
misguided friends and insidious enemies, that she does not
know what course to pursue in order to extricate herself from
the web of difficulties in which she seems almost hopelessly involved. In this dilemma she turns to me for help, and suppli-
cates for my guidance and instruction with a moving eloquence
that would touch the heart of a statue. Hear her sad story:

She says that when she was sixteen years old she met and

[*From* Sketches New and Old (1875).]

loved, with all the devotion of a passionate nature, a young man from New Jersey, named Williamson Breckinridge Caruthers, who was some six years her senior. They were engaged, with the free consent of their friends and relatives, and for a time it seemed as if their career was destined to be characterized by an immunity from sorrow beyond the usual lot of humanity. But at last the tide of fortune turned; young Caruthers became infected with smallpox of the most virulent type, and when he recovered from this illness his face was pitted like a waffle-mould, and his comeliness gone forever. Aurelia thought to break off the engagement at first, but pity for her unfortunate lover caused her to postpone the marriage-day for a season, and give him another trial.

The very day before the wedding was to have taken place, Breckinridge, while absorbed in watching the flight of a balloon, walked into a well and fractured one of his legs, and it had to be taken off above the knee. Again Aurelia was moved to break the engagement, but again love triumphed, and she set the day forward and gave him another chance to reform.

And again misfortune overtook the unhappy youth. He lost one arm by the premature discharge of a Fourth of July cannon, and within three months he got the other pulled out by a carding-machine. Aurelia's heart was almost crushed by these latter calamities. She could not but be deeply grieved to see her lover passing from her by piecemeal, feeling, as she did, that he could not last forever under this disastrous process of reduction, yet knowing of no way to stop its dreadful career, and in her tearful despair she almost regretted, like brokers who hold on and lose, that she had not taken him at first, before he had suffered such an alarming depreciation. Still, her brave soul bore her up, and she resolved to bear with her friend's unnatural disposition yet a little longer.

Again the wedding-day approached, and again disappointment overshadowed it; Caruthers fell ill with the erysipelas, and lost the use of one of his eyes entirely. The friends and relatives of the bride, considering that she had already put up with more than could reasonably be expected of her, now came forward and insisted that the match should be broken off; but after wavering a while, Aurelia, with a generous spirit which did her credit, said she had reflected calmly upon the matter, and could not discovered that Breckinridge was to blame.

So she extended the time once more, and he broke his other leg.

It was a sad day for the poor girl when she saw the surgeons reverently bearing away the sack whose uses she had learned by previous experience, and her heart told her the bitter truth that some more of her lover was gone. She felt that the field of her affections was growing more and more circumscribed every day, but once more she frowned down her relatives and renewed her betrothal.

Shortly before the time set for the nuptials another disaster occurred. There was but one man scalped by the Owens River Indians last year. That man was Williamson Breckinridge Caruthers of New Jersey. He was hurrying home with happiness in his heart, when he lost his hair forever, and in that hour of bitterness he almost cursed the mistaken mercy that had spared his head.

At last Aurelia is in serious perplexity as to what she ought to do. She still loves her Breckinridge, she writes, with truly womanly feeling—she still loves what is left of him—but her parents are bitterly opposed to the match, because he has no property and is disabled from working, and she has not sufficient means to support both comfortably. "Now, what should she do?" she asks with painful and anxious solicitude.

It is a delicate question; it is one which involves the life-long happiness of a woman, and that of nearly two-thirds of a man, and I feel that it would be assuming too great a responsibility to do more than make a mere suggestion in the case. How would it do to build to him? If Aurelia can afford the expense, let her furnish her mutilated lover with wooden arms and wooden legs, and a glass eye and a wig, and give him another show; give him ninety days, without grace, and if he does not break his neck in the meantime, marry him and take the chances. It does not seem to me that there is much risk, anyway, Aurelia, because if he sticks to his singular propensity for damaging himself every time he sees a good opportunity, his next experiment is bound to finish him, and then you are safe, married or single. If married, the wooden legs and such other valuables he may possess revert to the widow, and you see you sustain no actual loss save the fragment of a noble but most unfortunate husband, who honestly strove to do right, but whose extraordinary instincts were against him. Try it, Maria. I have thought the matter over carefully and well, and it is the only chance I see for you. It would have been a happy conceit on the part of Caruthers if he had started with his neck and broken that first; but since he has seen fit to choose a different policy and string himself out as long as possible, I do not think we ought to upbraid him for it if he has enjoyed it. We must do the best we can under the circumstances, and try not to feel exasperated at him.

PULVIS ET UMBRA

Robert Louis Stevenson

Robert Louis Stevenson (1850–1894), poet, novelist, essayist, and playwright, lived in an era which was dreadfully uncertain about the meaning of Man. The burgeoning role of science in the world —a role that gained new importance with the publication of the Origin of the Species in 1859—produced a great conflict between the older, romantic, and humanistic concept of life, and the newer, materialistic view. Out of this conflict came much fine writing, including Stevenson's "Pulvis et Umbra.[1]"

At first glance, the selection may seem more a formal than a familiar essay. But closer inspection will show that beneath the Biblical phrasing of the opening paragraph, the highly literate vocabulary of the remainder of the essay, and the studiedly simple style, there are a great many emotional undertones which reveal, as the Informal Essay best reveals, the personality and the reactions of the author.

We look for some reward of our endeavours and are disappointed; not success, not happiness, not even peace of conscience, crowns our ineffectual efforts to do well. Our frailties are invincible, our virtues barren; the battle goes sore against us to the going down of the sun. The canting moralist tells us of right and wrong; and we look abroad, even on the face of our small earth, and find them change with every climate, and no country where some action is not honoured for a virtue and none where it is not branded for a vice; and we look in our experience, and find no vital congruity in the wisest rules, but at the best a municipal fitness. It is not strange if we are tempted to despair of good. We ask too much. Our religions and moralities have

[*From* Across the Plains (*1892*).]

[1] Dust and Shadows.

been trimmed to flatter us, till they are all emasculate and senti-
mentalized, and only please and weaken. Truth is of a rougher
strain. In the harsh face of life, faith can read a bracing gospel.
The human race is a thing more ancient than the ten command-
ments; and the bones and revolutions of the Kosmos, in whose
joints we are but moss and fungus, more ancient still.

I

Of the Kosmos in the last resort, science reports many doubtful things and all of them appalling. There seems no substance
to this solid globe on which we stamp: nothing but symbols and
ratios. Symbols and ratios carry us and bring us forth and beat
us down; gravity that swings the incommensurable suns and
worlds through space, is but a figment varying inversely as the
squares of distances; and the suns and worlds themselves, im-
ponderable figures of abstraction, NH_3 and H_2O. Consideration
dares not dwell upon this view; that way madness lies; science
carries us into zones of speculation, where there is no habitable
city for the mind of man.

But take the Kosmos with a grosser faith, as our senses give it
us. We behold space sown with rotatory islands, suns and
worlds and the shards and wrecks of systems: some, like the sun,
still blazing; some rotting, like the earth; others, like the moon,
stable in desolation. All of these we take to be made of something we call matter: a thing which no analysis can help us to
conceive; to whose incredible properties no familiarities can
reconcile our minds. This stuff, when not purified by the lustra-
tion of fire, rots uncleanly into something we call life; seized
through all its atoms with a pediculous malady; swelling in
tumours that become independent, sometimes even (by an
abhorrent prodigy) locomotory; one splitting into millions, millions cohering into one, as the malady proceeds through varying stages. This vital putrescence of the dust, used as we are
to it, yet strikes us with occasional disgust, and the profusion
of worms in a piece of ancient turf, or the air of a marsh dark-
ened with insects, will sometimes check our breathing so that
we aspire for cleaner places. But none is clean: the moving

sand is infected with lice; the pure spring, where it bursts out of the mountain, is a mere issue of worms; even in the hard rock the crystal is forming.

In two main shapes this eruption covers the countenance of the earth: the animal and the vegetable: one in some degree the inversion of the other: the second rooted to the spot; the first coming detached out of its natal mud, and scurrying abroad with the myriad feet of insects, or towering into the heavens on the wings of birds,—a thing so incomprehensible that, if it be well considered, the heart stops. To what passes with the anchored vermin, we have little clue; doubtless they have their joys and sorrows, their delights and killing agonies,—it appears not how. But of the locomotory, to which we ourselves belong, we can tell more. These share with us a thousand miracles: the miracles of sight, of hearing, of the projection of sound, things that bridge space; the miracles of memory and reason, by which the present is conceived, and when it is gone its image kept living in the brains of man and brute; the miracle of reproduction, with its imperious desires and staggering consequences. And to put the last touch upon this mountain mass of the revolting and the inconceivable, all these prey upon each other, lives tearing other lives in pieces, cramming them inside themselves, and by that summary process growing fat: the vegetarian, the whale, perhaps the tree, not less than the lion of the desert, —for the vegetarian is only the eater of the dumb.

Meanwhile our rotary island loaded with predatory life, and more drenched with blood, both animal and vegetable, than ever mutinied ship, scuds through space with unimaginable speed, and turns alternate cheeks to the reverberation of a blazing world, ninety million miles away.

II

What a monstrous spectre is this man, the disease of the agglutinated dust, lifting alternate feet or lying drugged with slumber; killing, feeding, growing, bringing forth small copies of himself; grown upon with hair like grass, fitted with eyes that move and glitter in his face; a thing to set children screaming;

—and yet looked at earlier, known as his fellows know him, how surprising are his attributes! Poor soul, here for so little, cast among so many hardships, filled with desires so incommensurate and so inconsistent, savagely surrounded, savagely descended, irremediably condemned to prey upon his fellow lives: who should have blamed him had he been of a piece with his destiny and a being merely barbarous? And we look and behold him instead filled with imperfect virtues: infinitely childish, often admirably valiant, often touchingly kind; sitting down, amidst his momentary life, to debate of right and wrong and the attributes of the deity; rising up to do battle for an egg or die for an idea; singling out his friends and his mate with cordial affection; bringing forth in pain, rearing with long-suffering solicitude, his young. To touch the heart of his mystery, we find in him one thought, strange to the point of lunacy: the thought of duty; the thought of something owing to himself, to his neighbour, to his God: an ideal of decency, to which he would rise if it were possible; a limit of shame, below which, if it be possible, he will not stoop. The design in most men is one of conformity; here and there, in picked natures, it transcends itself and soars on the other side, arming martyrs with independence; but in all, in their degrees, it is a bosom thought: —not in man alone, for we trace it in dogs and cats whom we know fairly well, and doubtless some similar point of honour sways the elephant, the oyster, and the louse, of whom we know so little:—but in man, at least, it sways with so complete an empire that merely selfish things come second, even with the selfish; that appetites are starved, fears are conquered, pains supported; that almost the dullest shrinks from the reproof of a glance, although it were a child's; and all but the most cowardly stand amid the risks of war; and the more noble, having strongly conceived an act as due to their ideal, affront and embrace death. Strange enough if, with their singular origin and perverted practice, they think they are to be rewarded in some future life; strange still, if they are persuaded of the contrary, and think this blow which they solicit will strike them senseless for eternity. I shall be reminded what a tragedy of misconception and misconduct man at large presents,—of organized injustice, cowardly violence, and treacherous crime, and of the damning imperfections of the best. They cannot be too darkly drawn. Man is indeed marked for failure in his efforts to do right. But where the best consistently miscarry, how tenfold more remarkable that all should continue to strive; and surely we should find it both touching and inspiriting, that in a field from which success is banished, our race should not cease to labour.

If the first view of this creature, stalking in his rotatory isle, be a thing to shake the courage of the stoutest, on this nearer sight he startles us with an admiring wonder. It matters not where we look, under what climate we observe him, in what state of society, in what depth of ignorance, burthened with what erroneous morality; by camp-fires in Assiniboia, the snow powdering his shoulders, the wind plucking his blanket, as he sits passing the ceremonial calumet and uttering his grave opinions like a Roman senator; in ships at sea, a man inured to hardship and vile pleasures, his brightest hope a fiddle in a tavern and a bedizened trull who sells herself to rob him, and he for all that simple, innocent, cheerful, kindly like a child, constant to toil, brave to drown, for others; in the slums of cities, moving among indifferent millions to mechanical employment, without hope of change in the future, with scarce a pleasure in the present, and yet true to his virtues, honest up to his lights, kind to his neighbours, tempted perhaps in vain by the bright gin-palace, perhaps long-suffering with the drunken wife that ruins him; in India (a woman this time) kneeling with broken cries and streaming tears, as she drowns her child in the sacred river; in the brothel, the discard of society, living mainly on strong drink, fed with affronts, a fool, a thief, the comrade of thieves, and even here keeping the point of honour and the touch of pity, often repaying the world's scorn with service, often standing firm upon a scruple, and at a certain cost, rejecting riches:— everywhere some virtue cherished or affected, everywhere some decency of thought and carriage, everywhere the ensign of man's ineffectual goodness:—ah! if I could show you this! If I could show you these men and women, all the world over, in every stage of history, under every abuse of error, under every circumstance of failure, without hope, without help, without thanks, still obscurely fighting the lost fight of virtue, still clinging, in the brothel or on the scaffold, to some rag of honour, the poor jewel of their souls! They may seek to escape, and yet they cannot; it is not alone their privilege and glory, but their doom; they are condemned to some nobility; all their lives long, the desire of good is at their heels, the implacable hunter.

Of all earth's meteors, here at least is the most strange and consoling: That this ennobled lemur, this hair-crowned bubble of the dust, this inheritor of a few years and sorrows, should yet deny himself his rare delights, and add to his frequent pains, and live for an ideal, however misconceived. Nor can we stop with man. A new doctrine, received with screams a little while ago by canting moralists, and still not properly worked into the body of our thoughts, lights us a step farther into the heart of this rough but noble universe. For nowadays the pride of man denies in vain his kinship with the original dust. He stands no longer like a thing apart. Close at his heels we see the dog, prince of another genus: and in him too, we see dumbly testified the same cultus of an unattainable ideal, the same constancy in failure. Does it stop with the dog? We look at our feet where the ground is blackened with the swarming ant; a creature so small, so far from us in the hierarchy of brutes, that we can scarce trace and scarce comprehend his doings; and here also, in his ordered politics and rigorous justice, we see confessed the law of duty and the fact of individual sin. Does it stop, then, with the ant? Rather this desire of well-doing and this doom of frailty run through all the grades of life: rather is this earth, from the frosty top of Everest to the next margin of the internal fire, one stage of ineffectual virtues and one temple of pious tears and perseverance. The whole creation groaneth and travaileth together. It is the common and the god-like law of life. The browsers, the biters, the barkers, the hairy coats of field and forest, the squirrel in the oak, the thousand-footed creeper in the dust, as they share with us the gift of life, share with us the love of an ideal; strive like us—like us are tempted to grow weary of the struggle—to do well; like us receive at times unmerited refreshment, visitings of support, returns of courage; and are condemned like us to be crucified between that double law of the members and the will. Are they like us, I wonder, in the timid hope of some reward, some sugar with the drug? do they, too, stand aghast at unrewarded virtues, at the sufferings of those whom, in our partiality, we take to be just, and the prosperity of such as in our blindess we call wicked? It may be, and yet God knows what they should look for. Even while they look, even while they repent, the foot of man treads them by thousands in the dust, the yelping hounds burst upon their trail, the bullet speeds, the knives are heating in the den of the vivisectionist; or the dew falls, and the generation of a day is blotted out. For these are creatures compared with whom our weakness is strength, our ignorance wisdom, our brief span eternity.

And as we dwell, we living things in our isle of terror and under the imminent hand of death, God forbid it should be man the erected, the reasoner, the wise in his own eyes—God forbid it should be man that wearies in well-doing, that despairs of unrewarded effort, or utters the language of complaint. Let it be enough for faith, that the whole creation groans in mortal frailty, strives with unconquerable constancy: surely not all in vain.

THE CRIME

Max Beerbohm

*Sir Max Beerbohm (1872–1956), author, "caricaturist, and paro-
dist of genius," is most frequently anthologized today as a familiar
essayist, one whose gentle manner belies and gives force to the
keenness of his wit. In the nineties, he contributed to* The Yellow
Book *and* Vanity Fair, *and was thus associated with the preciosity
of this type of* fin de siècle *journalism. His total production in-
cludes seven volumes of collected caricatures, a collection of drama
reviews, a novel, and a number of volumes of essays and sketches.
Although he was at his best in oblique, suggestive essays, he once
said, "I wish I could cure myself of speaking ironically. I should
like to express myself in a straightforward manner."*

On a bleak wet stormy afternoon at the outset of last year's
spring, I was in a cottage, all alone, and knowing that I must be
all alone till evening. It was a remote cottage, in a remote
county, and had been 'let furnished' by its owner. My spirits
are easily affected by weather, and I hate solitude. And I dislike to be master of things that are not mine. 'Be careful not
to break us,' say the glass and china. 'You'd better not spill
ink on *me*,' growls the carpet. 'None of your dog's-earing,
thumb-marking, back-breaking tricks *here*,' snarl the books.

The books in this cottage looked particularly disagreeable—
horrid little upstarts of this and that scarlet or cerulean 'series'
of 'standard' authors. Having gloomily surveyed them, I turned
my back on them, and watched the rain streaming down the lat-
ticed window, whose panes seemed likely to be shattered at

any moment by the wind. I have known men who constantly visit the Central Criminal Court, visit also the scenes where famous crimes were committed, form their own theories of those crimes, collect souvenirs of those crimes, and call them-selves Criminologists. As for me, my interest in crime is, alas, merely morbid. I did not know, as those others would doubtless have known, that the situation in which I found myself was precisely of the kind most conducive to the darkest deeds. I did but bemoan it, and think of Lear in the hovel on the heath. The wind howled in the chimney, and the rain had begun to sputter right down it, so that the fire was beginning to hiss in a very sinister manner. Suppose the fire went out! It looked as if it meant to. I snatched the pair of bellows that hung beside it. I plied them vigorously. 'Now mind!—not *too* vigorously. We aren't yours!' they wheezed. I handled them more gently. But I did not release them till they had secured me a steady blaze.

I sat down before that blaze. Despair had been warded off. Gloom, however, remained; and gloom grew. I felt that I should prefer any one's thoughts to mine. I rose, I returned to the books. A dozen or so of those which were on the lowest of the three shelves were full-sized, were octavo, looked as though they had been bought to be read. I would exercise my un-doubted right to read one of them. Which of them? I grad-ually decided on a novel by a well-known writer whose works, though I had several times had the honour of meeting her, were known to me only by repute.

I knew nothing of them that was not good. The lady's 'out-put' had not been at all huge, and it was agreed that her 'level' was high. I had always gathered that the chief characteristic of her work was its great 'vitality.' The book in my hand was a third edition of her latest novel, and at the end of it were numer-ous press-notices, at which I glanced for confirmation. 'Im-mense vitality,' yes, said one critic. 'Full,' said another, 'of an intense vitality.' 'A book that will live,' said a third. How on earth did he know that? I was, however, very willing to believe in the vitality of this writer for all present purposes. Vitality

was a thing in which she herself, her talk, her glance, her ges-
tures, abounded. She and they had been, I remembered, rather
too much for me. The first time I met her, she said something
that I lightly and mildly disputed. On no future occasion did I
stem any opinion of hers. Not that she had been rude. Far
from it. She had but in a sisterly, brotherly way, and yet in a
way that was filially eager too, asked me to explain my point. I
did my best. She was all attention. But I was conscious that
my best, under her eye, was not good. She was quick to help
me: she said for me just what I had tried to say, and proceeded
to show me just why it was wrong. I smiled the gallant smile of
a man who regards women as all the more adorable because
logic is *not* their strong point, bless them! She asked—not ag-
gressively, but strenuously, as one who dearly loves a joke—
what I was smiling at. Altogether, a chastening encounter; and
my memory of it was tinged with a feeble resentment. How
she had scored! No man likes to be worsted in argument by a
woman. And I fancy that to be vanquished by a feminine
writer is the kind of defeat least of all agreeable to a man who
writes. A 'sex war,' we are often told, is to be one of the features
of the world's future—women demanding the right to do men's
work, and men refusing, resisting, counter-attacking. It seems
likely enough. One can believe anything of the world's future.
Yet one conceives that not all men, if this particular evil come
to pass, will stand packed shoulder to shoulder against all
women. One does not feel that the dockers will be very bitter
against such women as want to be miners, or the plumbers
frown much upon the would-be steeple-jills. I myself have
never had my sense of fitness jarred, nor a spark of animosity
roused in me, by a woman practising any of the fine arts—except the art of writing. That she should write a few little poems
or *pensées*, or some impressions of a trip in a dahabieh as far as
(say) Biskra, or even a short story or two, seems to me not
wholly amiss, even though she do such things for publication.
But that she should be an habitual, professional author, with
a passion for her art, and a fountain-pen and an agent, and sums
down in advance of royalties on sales in Canada and Australia,

and a profound knowledge of human character, and an essentially sane outlook, is somehow incongruous with my notions—
my mistaken notions, if you will—of what she ought to be.

'Has a profound knowledge of human character, and an essentially sane outlook,' said one of the critics quoted at the end
of the book that I had chosen. The wind and the rain in the
chimney had not abated, but the fire was bearing up bravely. So
would I. I would read cheerfully and without prejudice. I
poked the fire and, pushing my chair slightly back, lest the heat
should warp the book's covers, began Chapter 1. A woman sat
writing in a summer-house at the end of a small garden that
overlooked a great valley in Surrey. The description of her was
calculated to make her very admirable—a thorough *woman*, not
strictly beautiful, but likely to be thought beautiful by those
who knew her well; not dressed as though she gave much heed
to her clothes, but dressed in a fashion that exactly harmonized
with her special type. Her pen 'travelled' rapidly across the
foolscap, and while it did so she was described in more and
more detail. But at length she came to a 'knotty point' in what
she was writing. She paused, she pushed back the hair from her
temples, she looked forth at the valley; and now the landscape
was described, but not at all exhaustively, for the writer soon
overcame her difficulty, and her pen travelled faster than ever,
till suddenly there was a cry of 'Mammy!' and in rushed a seven-
year-old child, in conjunction with whom she was more than
ever admirable; after which the narrative skipped back across
eight years, and the woman became a girl, giving as yet no token
of future eminence in literature, but—I had an impulse which I
obeyed almost before I was conscious of it.

Nobody could have been more surprised than I was at what
I had done—done so neatly, so quietly and gently. The book
stood closed, upright, with its back to me, just as on a book-
shelf, behind the bars of the grate. There it was. And it gave
forth, as the flames crept up the blue cloth sides of it, a pleasant
though acrid smell. My astonishment had passed, giving place
to an exquisite satisfaction. How pottering and fumbling a
thing was even the best kind of written criticism! I understood

the contempt felt by the man of action for the man of words. But what pleased me most was that at last, actually, I, at my age, I of all people, had committed a crime—was guilty of a crime. I had power to revoke it. I might write to my book-seller for an unburnt copy, and place it on the shelf where this one had stood—this gloriously glowing one. I would do nothing of the sort. What I had done I had done. I would wear for ever on my conscience the white rose of theft and the red rose of arson. If hereafter the owner of this cottage happened to miss that volume—let him! If he were fool enough to write to me about it, would I share my grand secret with him? No. Gently, with his poker, I prodded that volume further among the coals. The all-but-consumed binding shot forth little tongues of bright colour—flamelets of sapphire, amethyst, emerald. Charming! Could even the author herself not admire them? Perhaps. Poor woman!—I had scored now, scored so perfectly that I felt myself to be almost a brute while I poked off the loosened black outer pages and led the fire on to pages that were but pale brown.

These were quickly devoured. But it seemed to me that whenever I left the fire to forage for itself it made little head-way. I pushed the book over on its side. The flames closed on it, but presently, licking their lips, fell back, as though they had had enough. I took the tongs and put the book upright again, and raked it fore and aft. It seemed almost as thick as ever. With poker and tongs I carved it into two, three sections—the inner pages flashing white as when they were sent to the bind-ers. Strange! Aforetime, a book was burnt now and again in the market-place by the common hangman. Was he, I won-dered, paid by the hour? I had always supposed the thing quite easy for him—a bright little, brisk little conflagration, and so home. Perhaps other books were less resistant than this one? I began to feel that the critics were more right than they knew. Here was a book that had indeed an intense vitality, and an immense vitality. It was a book that would live—do what one might. I vowed it should not. I subdivided it, spread it, redis-tributed it. Ever and anon my eye would be caught by some

sentence or fragment of a sentence in the midst of a charred
page before the flames crept over it. 'lways loathed you, bu,' I
remember; and 'ning. Tolstoy was right.' Who had always
loathed whom? And what, what, had Tolstoy been right about?
I had an absurd but genuine desire to know. Too late! Con-
found the woman!—she was scoring again. I furiously drove
her pages into the yawning crimson jaws of the coals. Those
jaws had lately been golden. Soon, to my horror, they seemed
to be growing grey. They seemed to be closing—on nothing.
Flakes of black paper, full-sized layers of paper brown and white,
began to hide them from me altogether. I sprinkled a boxful
of wax matches. I resumed the bellows. I lunged with the
poker. I held a newspaper over the whole grate. I did all that
inspiration could suggest, or skill accomplish. Vainly. The fire
went out—darkly, dismally, gradually, quite out.

How she had scored again! But she did not know it. I felt no
bitterness against her as I lay back in my chair, inert, listening to
the storm that was still raging. I blamed only myself. I had
done wrong. The small room became very cold. Whose fault
was that but my own? I had done wrong hastily, but had done
it and been glad of it. I had not remembered the words a wise
king wrote long ago, that the lamp of the wicked shall be put
out, and that the way of transgressors is hard.

THIS BODY

Robert Lynd

Robert Lynd (1879–1949) is one of the few accomplished essayists who have written in no other form. He began his career as a journalist, specializing in literary criticism and light essays, and quickly became one of the earliest and the most popular of the British newspaper columnists. Although he was an extremely prolific writer, his essays have not yet been collected. This probably accounts for the fact that he is much better known and respected in England than in the United States.

Desmond Perkins once remarked that "Lynd understood well that the art of the essayist is to find little by-paths . . . leading out of the thoroughfare of every-day interests into the gardens of fancy and thought." The following essay is such an excursion, invested with both meaning and charm in the best tradition of the Informal Essay.

There are occasional items of news in the papers that pull us up and tempt us to examine our attitude in regard to some question as if for the first time. One item of the kind was the announcement of the will of Edward Martyn, Irish revivalist and cousin of Mr. George Moore, in accordance with which his dead body was to be given to a medical school for dissection and the remains were afterwards to be buried, like other dissecting-room corpses, in a pauper's grave. Who, on reading this, could fail to turn round and ask himself whether he could endure the prospect of his body's being subjected, though past sense, to the knives of medical students? There are few people, indeed, who could be entirely indifferent on such a matter. If a man is careless of the fate of his body after death, as Socrates

[*From* The Peal of Bells *by Robert Lynd, Methuen and Company Ltd.; reprinted by permission of the executors of the estate of Robert Lynd, the publishers, and the author's daughter.*]

was, it is thought a sufficiently remarkable fact to be preserved in his biography. Christians ought, perhaps, of all people to have been most able to achieve this happy carelessness. But even the belief in the immortality of the soul has seldom persuaded human beings that a dead body is as worthless as the husk of a seed that has burst out of darkness into a flower. In the result, Christians have for centuries paid honour to dead bodies as though they were more noble than the living, and many a poor man has never had the hats of passers-by raised to him till he has driven through the streets as a corpse. I do not know how far modern Christians believe that after long ages at the sound of a trumpet the body that has been the prey of worms and of dusty time will actually rise out of the earth, recomposed into the likeness of a living man. Probably there are few who would now confess to any certainty about the matter. But many good men in the past believed that the dead body, far from being a worthless garment that the soul had cast off for ever, was the very garment that the soul would resume on its exaltation into Paradise. Even those Christians who despised the body alive glorified it in death, and a saint's body that he had kept starved and unclean as beneath contempt was revered after death as something with a divine power to perform miracles. This may seem, and is, paradoxical, but the awe of the living in presence of a dead body is natural to reflecting men. Certain savages, we are told, pay honour to the bodies of the dead only because they fear that, if they do not, the spirits of the dead will haunt them. But the civilised man, who has no such terrors, is as reverent because, perhaps, he sees in the dead body a sign and wonder that changes the aspect of the world for him and brings him to the very door of the mystery of his own life.

Whatever be the reason, the world has not yet outgrown the feeling that the dead must be honoured and not treated as refuse. The outcry during the War against the supposed German 'corpse-factory,' in which dead soldiers were turned into useful oils or chemicals for the munition factories, was something more than an expression of propagandist hypocrisy.

It was absurd to believe that the Germans, being human beings, would sanction such a thing; but it was natural to believe that, if they did, they would themselves be so much the less human beings. And yet, if it is right to use a dead man's body for purposes of medicine, there is no logical reason why it should be a crime to use a dead man's body for purposes of war. It is arguable, indeed, that the needs of war are the more urgent, and that therefore the 'corpse-factory' should be less horrifying to us than the dissecting-room. As a matter of fact, the dissecting-room would horrify us a great deal more if it were not that we have nationalised (or municipalised) the bodies of friendless paupers. When anatomists sent their scouts into the graveyards to dig up the dead who had died solvent, the friends of the dead leagued themselves together and guarded the body by night till it had rotted in the earth. How many of us in our childhood grew up amid a thousand-and-one tales of body-snatchers! What devils they and the kidnappers seemed! How thrilling to hear of their adventures! We might laugh at them, as at the crimes of Bluebeard, but we laughed uneasily. Yet in another thousand years men may be looking back on the body-snatchers and kidnappers as among the saints of science, and Burke and Hare may be honoured as martyrs. I do not think they will, but it is possible at least that science progressed as a result of their crimes. There is certainly as much to be said in reason for allowing the dissecting-room to choose its bodies casually from the graveyards as for giving it the right to use its lancets on the unclaimed bodies of paupers. But, as most of us hope that neither we nor our friends will end even in these costly days in the workhouse, we are content with the present compromise, and we scarcely ask ourselves how the dissecting-rooms are to be supplied when poverty has been abolished. No doubt there will always be enough men and women with such religious devotion to science that they will volunteer for the dissecting-room in their wills. But our first instinct, if volunteers were called for, would be to shrink as if from a painful sacrifice.

I, for one, should find it difficult to bequeath my body into the reckless hands of medical students. I do not know why, except that I cannot help somehow or other identifying my body with myself. Socrates was philosopher enough, on the eve of his death, to see his body as a shell and to say to himself: 'That is not I.' Most of us, however, though we might admit in our intelligences that our bodies were not we, would continue to think of them as ourselves in our imaginations. Whatever our essence, it is through the body that we have visited the earth, and we cannot dissociate from it any of the experiences that have made life so well worth living that we wish to go on with it. Our body was at least our inseparable consort, whether we went to church or to the tavern, whether we found our happiness in the sunny waist of the earth or by a coal fire at home, whether we played in the nursery or were kings of the football field, or fell in love or were rewarded with the great public prizes of the world. There has not been a single experience of our lives that would have been possible without hands, feet, heart, lungs, brain, mouth, eyes and ears. It is no wonder that St. Francis, on his death-bed, apologised to his body for having used it so ill, for without it there would have been no St. Francis, and the birds would have gone without their only sermon. How, then, can we be indifferent to such an associate? If a church made from the stones of the hills becomes sacred through associations, so that men, on entering it, take off their hats out of reverence for the temple of God, how much less surprising is it that a man should take thought for the fate of his body that is made of flesh and bones? Many men even leave instructions that honours shall be paid to their dead bodies such as they never demanded during life, like the Ulster Unionist who asked that his body should be wrapped in a Union Jack and taken out and buried in Britannia's sea. Others have died the more easily because they knew that their remains (as the phrase goes) would be buried in some particular place —on the top of a hill, or in a cemetery with ghostly headstones visible from the sea at evening, or under the trees by an old church in a half-deserted village. I myself should feel melancholy if I thought I was to be buried in the Sahara or even in one of the colonies, and for a long time I should have felt a sharp pang if it had been foretold that I should be buried anywhere except in my own country, and I was particular even as to the exact spot in that. I do not know if I care so much as I once did. I fancy I have a growing objection to being buried anywhere at all. Nor do I take to the prospect of being burned. So long as one thinks of one's body as a living thing, one can hardly imagine an end to it that does not seem almost as horrible as the dissecting-table. To be perpetuated as a mummy—who would care for that? Better to be cleansed swiftly by the earth into a skeleton in a Christian grave. When I had just left school and thought I was a pantheist, I used to take a sentimental pleasure, as other boys have done, in the prospect that flowers would spring from my tomb. I even liked the thought that I should help to fertilise the earth for those flowers. I cannot comfort myself so easily now, though I should be the happier if I thought the gardener would occasionally pay some small attention to my coverture. But I have really no taste for the underworld, and, if it were possible, I do not think I should ever visit it, but should continue on the floor of this excellent earth as long as the Wandering Jew. It is said that in the end men grow tired of the body, and are glad enough to leave it. Those who do, I fancy, are bolder spirits than I. I am naturally a stay-at-home, and the only home in which I have lived all my life is my body. Born under Saturn, I have nevertheless been happy enough never to wish to change it for a better. If I have wished to be a better man, I have still wished for the new spirit to inhabit the same body, for, though it is a body that no man could be proud of, not being built in any of the noble styles of architecture, I am used to it and am bound to it by all manner of sympathies. Not that I have looked after it as well as I might have done. I have allowed it to sink into dilapidation and disrepair, so that it already resembles more than it should a piece of antiquity. But even the crooked man with the crooked cat probably lived happily enough in his crooked little house, and would not have left it without compulsion. Hence, though I cannot share their faith,

I should not be sorry to think that those Christians were right
who believe that on the last day the body will be whisked
through the air to become the house of the soul again in a
better world. I do not defend myself or pretend that this is a
laudable attitude. I admire Socrates, indeed, and all those who
have despised the body as a fragile pot or as grass that withers,
but I cannot help recognising the fact that I am not of their
company.

On the other hand, I cannot go so far as those people who
shrink from the grave all the more because they cannot endure
the thought of the rain beating down upon them by night and
chilling their senseless bones. I read somewhere lately that,
when the woman he loved died, Abraham Lincoln was almost
driven mad during a storm by the feeling that the wind was
howling and the rain falling on her grave. Others have told
me that they share this feeling, and I know a man who said
that he would hate to be buried in a certain graveyard because
it was 'very damp.' But then he was subject to rheumatism.
His objection was as valid, however, as is the objection of most
of us to lie, misshapen and skinny, under the eyes of a professor
on the dissecting-table. We impute to our dead bodies many of
the senses and shames of the living, and we shudder without
reason at the thought of things occurring to them that could
injure us only while we are alive. Thus do we give ourselves
an extension of life in our fancies. It seems as though we must
be surer that life is worth living than that death is worth dying.
But, even on this matter, there is room for hope.

THE AUTHOR AT WORK

H. L. Mencken

H. L. Mencken (1880–1956), editor, essayist, and critic, was one of the major influences on American literature in the second and third decades of this century. As editor of Smart Set *and of* The American Mercury, *he was in a position to support and encourage other writers who, like himself, were attacking the complacency and sterile culture of American society.*

As a writer, Mencken was renowned for his wit, his censor baiting, and his inimitable use of irony and invective. He was a formidable man who wielded a formidable pen; and like Robert Lynd he realized that his ideas were best expressed in the Informal Essay. But, iconoclastic essayist though he was, he was also capable of writing The American Language (1919), *one of the best treatments of our language in the tradition of modern philology and linguistic history.*

The following essay shows Mencken's vigorous command of the language, his humorous but knife-sharp criticism, his technique of overstatement used to make his point.

If authors could work in large, well-ventilated factories, like cigarmakers or garment-workers, with plenty of their mates about and a flow of lively professional gossip to entertain them, their labor would be immensely lighter. But it is essential to their craft that they perform its tedious and vexatious operations *a cappella*, and so the horrors of loneliness are added to stenosis and their other professional infirmities. An author at work is continuously and inescapably in the presence of himself. There is nothing to divert and soothe him. Every time a vagrant regret or sorrow assails him, it has him instantly by the ear, and every time a wandering ache runs down his leg it shakes him like the bite of a tiger. I have yet to meet an author who was not a hypochondriac. Saving only medical men, who are always ill and in fear of death, the literati are perhaps the most lavish consumers of pills and philtres in this world, and the most assiduous customers of surgeons. I can scarcely think of one, known to me personally, who is not constantly dosing himself with medicines, or regularly resorting to the knife.

It must be obvious that other men, even among the intelligentsia, are not beset so cruelly. A judge on the bench, entertaining a ringing in the ears, can do his work quite as well as if he heard only the voluptuous rhetoric of the lawyers. A clergyman, carrying on his mummery, is not appreciably crippled by a sour stomach: what he says has been said before, and only scoundrels question it. And a surgeon, plying his exhilarating art and mystery, suffers no professional damage from the wild thought that the attending nurse is more sightly than his wife. But I defy anyone to write a competent sonnet with a ringing in his ears, or to compose sound criticism with a sour stomach, or to do a plausible love scene with a head full of private amorous fancies. These things are sheer impossibilities. The poor literatus encounters them and their like every time he enters his work-room and spits on his hands. The moment the door bangs he begins a depressing, losing struggle with his body and his mind.

Why then, do rational men and women engage in so barbarous and exhausting a vocation—for there are relatively intelligent and enlightened authors, remember, just as there are relatively honest politicians, and even bishops. What keeps them from deserting it for trades that are less onerous, and, in the eyes of their fellow creatures, more respectable? One reason, I believe, is that an author, like any other so-called artist, is a man in whom the normal vanity of all men is so vastly exaggerated that he finds it a sheer impossibility to hold it in. His overpowering impulse is to gyrate before his fellow men, flapping his wings and emitting defiant yells. This being forbidden by the police of all civilized countries, he takes it out by putting his yells on paper. Such is the thing called self-expression.

In the confidences of the literati, of course, it is always depicted as something much more mellow and virtuous. Either they argue that they are moved by a yearning to spread the enlightenment and save the world, or they allege that what steams them and makes them leap is a passion for beauty. Both theories are quickly disposed of by an appeal to the facts. The stuff written by nine authors out of ten, it must be plain at a glance, has as little to do with spreading the enlightenment as the state papers of the late Chester A. Arthur. And there is no more beauty in it, and no more sign of a feeling of beauty, than you will find in the décor of a night-club. The impulse to create beauty, indeed, is rather rare in literary men, and almost completely absent from the younger ones. If it shows itself at all, it comes as a sort of afterthought. Far ahead of it comes the yearning to make money. And after the yearning to make money comes the yearning to make a noise. The impulse to create beauty lingers far behind. Authors, as a class, are extraordinarily insensitive to it, and the fact reveals itself in their customary (and often incredibly extensive) ignorance of the other arts. I'd have a hard job naming six American novelists who could be depended upon to recognize a fugue without prompting, or six poets who could give a rational account of the difference between a Gothic cathedral and a Standard Oil filling-station.

The thing goes even further. Most novelists, in my experience, know nothing of poetry, and very few poets have any feeling for the beauties of prose. As for the dramatists, three-fourths of them are unaware that such things as prose and poetry exist at all. It pains me to set down such inconvenient and blushful facts. If they ought to be concealed, then blame my babbling upon scientific passion. That passion, today, has me by the ear.

INDIANS AND ENTERTAINMENT

D. H. Lawrence

D. H. Lawrence (1885–1930), novelist, poet, essayist, and play-wright, has been the subject of much controversy. Most popularly known as a novelist, he is also one of the finest of essayists, especially in the genre of the informal travel essay.

Lawrence rebelled against both the social system and the industrial civilization of the twentieth century, and attempted, in his writing, to show the need for a fuller and more intense life to express one's own individuality and that of one's culture. Mornings in Mexico (1927), from which "Indians and Entertainment," is taken, is Lawrence's picture of the Indian's basic struggle with life on his native plain. The essay, which clearly shows Lawrence's concern with the "life-impulse," might best be compared to Huxley's essay on Central America (p. 115) in order to see the difference between a writer who approaches his material primarily from an emotional viewpoint—as Lawrence does—and one who approaches it primarily from an intellectual viewpoint, as Huxley does.

Perhaps the commonest entertainment among the Indians is singing round the drum, at evening, when the day is over. European peasants will sit round the fire and sing. But they sing ballads or lyrics, tales about individuals or individual, personal experience. And each individual identifies the emotion of the song with his own emotion.

Or the wild fishermen of the Outer Hebrides will sing in their intense, concentrated way, by the fire. And again, usually, the songs have words. Yet sometimes not. Sometimes the song has merely sounds, and a marvellous melody. It is the seal drifting in to shore on the wave, or the seal-woman, singing low and secret, departing back from the shores of men, through the surf, back to the realm of the outer beasts that rock on the waters and stare through glistening, vivid, mindless eyes.

This is approaching the Indian song. But even this is pictorial, conceptual far beyond the Indian point. The Hebridean still sees himself human, and *outside* the great naturalistic influences, which are the dramatic circumstances of his life.

The Indian, singing, sings without words or vision. Face lifted and sightless, eyes half closed and visionless, mouth open and speechless, the sounds arise in his chest, from the consciousness in the abdomen. He will tell you it is a song of a man coming home from the bear-hunt: or a song to make rain: or a song to make the corn grow: or even, quite modern, the song of the church bell on Sunday morning.

By the man coming home from the bear-hunt is any man, all men, the bear is any bear, every bear, all bear. There is no individual, isolated experience. It is the hunting, tired, triumphant demon of manhood which has won against the squint-eyed demon of all bears. The experience is generic, non-individual. It is an experience of the human blood-stream, not of the mind or spirit. Hence the subtle incessant, insistent rhythm of the drum, which is pulsated like the heart, and soulless, and unescapable. Hence the strange blind unanimity of the Indian men's voices. The experience is one experience, tribal, of the blood-stream. Hence, to our ears, the absence of melody. Melody is individualized emotion, just as orchestral music is the harmonizing again of many separate, individual emotions or experiences. But the real Indian song is non-individual, and without melody. Strange, clapping, crowing, gurgling sounds, is an unseizable subtle rhythm, the rhythm of the heart in her throes: from a parted entranced mouth, from a chest powerful and free, from an abdomen where the great blood-stream surges in the dark, and surges in its own generic experiences.

This may mean nothing to you. To the ordinary white ear, the Indian's singing is a rather disagreeable howling of dogs to a tom-tom. But if it rouses no other sensation, it rouses a touch of fear amid hostility. Whatever the spirit of man may be, the blood is basic.

Or take the song to make the corn grow. The dark faces stoop forward, in a strange race darkness. The eyelashes droop a little in the dark, ageless, vulnerable faces. The drum is a heart beating with insistent thuds. And the spirits of the men go out on the ether, vibrating in waves from the hot, dark, intentional blood, seeking the creative presence that hovers forever in one ether, seeking the identification, following on down the mysterious rhythms of the creative pulse, on and on into the germinating quick of the maize that lies under the ground, there, with the throbbing, pulsing, clapping rhythm that comes from the dark, creative blood in man, to stimulate the tremulous, pulsating protoplasm in the seed-germ, till it throws forth its rhythms of creative energy into rising blades of leaf and stem.

JAMES WOODFORDE

Virginia Woolf

Virginia Woolf (1882–1941), novelist and essayist, was the daughter of the great English critic and historian, Sir Leslie Stephen. She was related to the Darwins, the Stracheys, and the Thackerays, and her family included in its close social circle such men as R. L. Stevenson, Thomas Hardy, James Russell Lowell, and John Ruskin.

As a novelist, she is distinguished by her concern for what Stanley Kunitz calls "the single instant and the mysterious relation which seems to link events occurring apart." This concern with time, which she felt to be the primary matter of the novel, is shown in her best novels, Mrs. Dalloway (1925) and To the Lighthouse (1927). This attitude is also part of her essays, which attempt to create a man or an age by the "single instant," by the detail which gives to the subject reality and humanity. The Common Reader, from which the following essay is taken, is addressed not to the scholar or the critic, but to the common reader: he who reads for pleasure. With her ability to recreate the past, with her delicate style which gives to her writings a vivifying touch, Mrs. Woolf provides that pleasure.

One could wish that the psycho-analysts would go into the question of diary-keeping. For often it is the one mysterious fact in a life otherwise as clear as the sky and as candid as the dawn. Parson Woodforde[1] is a case in point—his diary is the only mystery about him. For forty-three years he sat down almost daily to record what he did on Monday and what he had for dinner on Tuesday; but for whom he wrote or why he wrote it is impossible to say. He does not unburden his soul

[*From* The Second Common Reader *by Virginia Woolf, copyright, 1932, by Harcourt, Brace and Company, Inc. Reprinted by permission of the publishers and Leonard Woolf.*]

[1] 1740–1803.

in his diary; yet it is no mere record of engagements and expenses. As for literary fame, there is no sign that he ever thought of it, and finally, though the man himself is peaceable above all things, there are little indiscretions and criticisms which would have got him into trouble and hurt the feelings of his friends had they read them. What purpose, then, did the sixty-eight little books fulfil? Perhaps it was the desire for intimacy. When James Woodforde opened one of his neat manuscript books he entered into conversation with a second James Woodforde, who was not quite the same as the reverend gentleman who visited the poor and preached in the church. These two friends said much that all the world might hear; but they had a few secrets which they shared with each other only. It was a great comfort, for example, that Christmas when Nancy, Betsy, and Mr. Waler seemed to be in conspiracy against him, to exclaim in the diary, "The treatment I meet with for my Civility this Christmas is to me abominable." The second James Woodforde sympathised and agreed. Again, when a stranger abused his hospitality it was a relief to inform the other self who lived in the little book that he had put him to sleep in the attic story, "and I treated him as one that would be too free if treated kindly." It is easy to understand why, in the quite life of a country parish, these two bachelor friends became in time inseparable. An essential part of him would have died had he been forbidden to keep his diary. When indeed he thought himself in the grip of death he still wrote on and on. And as we read—if reading is the word for it—we seem to be listening to some one who is murmuring over the events of the day to himself in the quiet space which precedes sleep. It is not writing, and, to speak of the truth, it is not reading. It is slipping through half a dozen pages and strolling to the window and looking out. It is going on thinking about the Woodfordes while we watch the people in the street below. It is taking a walk and making up the life and character of James Woodforde as we go. It is not reading any more than it is writing—what to call it we scarcely know.

James Woodforde, then, was one of those smooth-cheeked,

steady-eyed men, demure to look at, whom we can never imagine except in the prime of life. He was of an equable temper,
with only such acerbities and touchinesses as are generally to be
found in those who have had a love affair in their youth and
remained, as they fancy, unwed because of it. The Parson's
love affair, however, was nothing very tremendous. Once when
he was a young man in Somerset he liked to walk over to
Shepton and to visit a certain "sweet tempered" Betsy White
who lived there. He had a great mind "to make a bold stroke"
and ask her to marry him. He went so far, indeed, as to pro-
pose marriage "when opportunity served," and Betsy was willing.
But he delayed; time passed; four years passed indeed, and
Betsy went to Devonshire, met a Mr. Webster, who had five
hundred pounds a year, and married him. When James Woodforde met them in the turnpike road he could say little, "being
shy," but to his diary he remarked—and this no doubt was his
private version of the affair ever after—"she has proved herself
to me a mere jilt."

But he was a young man then, and as time went on we
cannot help suspecting that he was glad to consider the question of marriage shelved once and for all so that he might
settle down with his niece Nancy at Weston Longueville, and
give himself simply and solely, every day and all day, to the
great business of living. Again, what else to call it we do not
know.

For James Woodforde was nothing in particular. Life had it
all her own way with him. He had no special gift; he had no
oddity or infirmity. It is idle to pretend that he was a zealous
priest. God in Heaven was much the same to him as King
George upon the throne—a kindly Monarch, that is to say,
whose festivals one kept by preaching a sermon on Sunday
much as one kept the Royal birthday by firing a blunderbuss
and drinking a toast at dinner. Should anything untoward
happen, like the death of a boy who was dragged and killed
by a horse, he would instantly, but rather perfunctorily exclaim,
"I hope to God the Poor Boy is happy," and add, "We all
came home singing"; just as when Justice Creed's peacock spread

its tail—"and most noble it is"—he would exclaim, "How
wonderful are Thy Works O God in every Being." But there
was no fanaticism, no enthusiasm, no lyric impulse about James
Woodforde. In all these pages, indeed, each so neatly divided
into compartments, and each of those again filled, as the days
themselves were filled, quietly and fully in a hand steady as
the pacing of a well-tempered nag, one can only call to mind
a single poetic phrase about the transit of Venus. "It appeared
as a black patch upon a fair Lady's face," he says. The words
themselves are mild enough, but they hang over the undulating
expanse of the Parson's prose with the resplendence of the star
itself. So in the Fen country a barn or a tree appears twice its
natural size against the surrounding flats. But what led him to
this palpable excess that summer's night we cannot tell. It
cannot have been that he was drunk. He spoke out too roundly
against such failings in his brother Jack to be guilty himself.
Temperamentally he was among the eaters of meat and not
among the drinkers of wine. When we think of the Woodfordes, uncle and niece, we think of them as often as not waiting with some impatience for their dinner. Gravely they watch
the joint as it is set upon the table; swiftly they get their knives
to work upon the succulent leg or loin; without much comment,
unless a word is passed about the gravy or the stuffing, they
go on eating. So they munch, day after day, year in year out,
until between them they must have devoured herds of sheep
and oxen, flocks of poultry, an odd dozen or so of swans and
cygnets, bushels of apples and plums, while the pastries and the
jellies crumble and squash beneath their spoons in mountains,
in pyramids, in pagodas. Never was there a book so stuffed
with food as this one is. To read the bill of fare respectfully
and punctually set forth gives one a sense of repletion. Trout
and chicken, mutton and peas, pork and apple sauce—so the
joints succeed each other at dinner, and there is supper with
more joints still to come, all, no doubt, home grown, and of
the juiciest and sweetest; all cooked, often by the mistress
herself, in the plainest English way, save when the dinner was
at Weston Hall and Mrs. Custance surprised them with a Lon-

don dainty—a pyramid of jelly, that is to say, with a "landscape appearing through it." After dinner sometimes, Mrs. Custance, for whom James Woodforde had a chivalrous devotion, would play the "Sticcardo Pastorale," and make "very soft music indeed"; or would get out her work-box and show them how neatly contrived it was, unless indeed she were giving birth to another child upstairs. These infants the Parson would baptize and very frequently he would bury them. They died almost as frequently as they were born. The Parson had a deep respect for the Custances. They were all that country gentry should be—a little given to the habit of keeping mistresses, perhaps, but that pecadillo could be forgiven them in view of their generosity to the poor, the kindness they showed to Nancy, and their condescension in asking the Parson to dinner when they had great people staying with them. Yet great people were not much to James's liking. Deeply though he respected the nobility, "one must confess," he said, "that being with our equals is much more agreeable."

Not only did Parson Woodforde know what was agreeable; that rare gift was by the bounty of Nature supplemented by another equally rare—he could have what he wanted. The age was propitious. Monday, Tuesday, Wednesday—they follow each other and each little compartment seems filled with content. The days were not crowded, but they were enviably varied. Fellow of New College though he was, he did things with his own hands, not merely with his own head. He lived in every room of the house—in the study he wrote sermons, in the dining-room he ate copiously; he cooked in the kitchen, he played cards in the parlour. And then he took his coat and stick and went coursing his greyhounds in the fields. Year in, year out, the provisioning of the house and its defence against the cold of winter and the drought of summer fell upon him. Like a general he surveyed the seasons and took steps to make his own little camp safe with coal and wood and beef and beer against the enemy. His day thus had to accommodate a jumble of incongruous occupations. There is religion to be served, and the pig to be killed; the sick to be visited and dinner

to be eaten; the dead to be buried and beer to be brewed;
Convocation to be attended and the cow to be bolused. Life
and death, mortality and immorality, jostle in his pages and
make a good mixed marriage of it: ". . . found the old gentleman almost at his last gasp. Totally senseless with rattlings in
his Throat. Dinner today boiled beef and Rabbit rosted." All
is as it should be; life is like that.

Surely, surely, then, here is one of the breathing-spaces in
human affairs—here in Norfolk at the end of the eighteenth
century at the Parsonage. For once man is content with his
lot; harmony is achieved; his house fits him; a tree is a tree;
a chair is a chair; each knows its office and fulfils it. Looking
through the eyes of Parson Woodforde, the different lives of
men seem orderly and settled. Far away guns roar; a King
falls; but the sound is not loud enough to scare the rooks here
in Norfolk. The proportions of things are different. The Continent is so distant that it looks a mere blur; America scarcely
exists; Australia is unknown. But a magnifying glass is laid
upon the fields of Norfolk. Every blade of grass is visible there.
We see every lane and every field; the ruts on the roads and
the peasants' faces. Each house stands in its own breadth of
meadow isolated and independent. No wires link village to
village. No voices thread the air. The body also is more present
and more real. It suffers more acutely. No anaesthetic deadens
physical pain. The surgeon's knife hovers real and sharp above
the limb. Cold strikes unmitigated upon the house. The milk
freezes in the pans; the water is thick with ice in the basins.
One can scarcely walk from one room to another in the parsonage in winter. Poor men and women are frozen to death upon
the roads. Often no letters come and there are no visitors and
no newspapers. The Parsonage stands alone in the midst of the
frost-bound fields. At last, Heaven be praised, life circulates
again; a man comes to the door with a Madagascar monkey; another brings a box containing a child with two distinct perfect
heads; there is a rumour that a balloon is going to rise at Norwich. Every little incident stands out sharp and clear. The drive
to Norwich even is something of an adventure. One must trun-

dle every step of the way behind a horse. But look how distinct the trees stand in the hedges; how slowly the cattle move their heads as the carriage trots by; how gradually the spires of Norwich raise themselves above the hill. And then how clear-cut and familiar are the faces of the few people who are our friends —the Custances, Mr. du Quesne. Friendship has time to solidify, to become a lasting, a valuable possession.

True, Nancy of the younger generation is visited now and then by a flighty notion that she is missing something, that she wants something. One day she complained to her uncle that life was very dull: she complained "of the dismal situation of my house, nothing to be seen, and little or no visiting or being visited, &c.," and made him very uneasy. We could read Nancy a little lecture upon the folly of wanting that "et cetera." Look what your "et cetera" has brought to pass, we might say; half the countries of Europe are bankrupt; there is a red line of villas on every green hillside; your Norfolk roads are black as tar; there is no end to "visiting or being visited." But Nancy has an answer to make us, to the effect that our past is her present. You, she says, think it a great privilege to be born in the eighteenth century, because one called cowslips pagles and rode in a curricle instead of driving in a car. But you are utterly wrong, you fanatical lovers of memoirs, she goes on. I can assure you, my life was often intolerably dull. I did not laugh at the things that make you laugh. It did not amuse me when my uncle dreamt of a hat or saw bubbles in the beer, and said that meant a death in the family; I thought so too. Betsy Davy mourned young Walker with all her heart in spite of dressing in sprigged paduasoy. There is a great deal of humbug talked of the eighteenth century. Your delight in old times and old diaries is half impure. You make up something that never had any existence. Our sober reality is only a dream to you— so Nancy grieves and complains, living through the eighteenth century day by day, hour by hour.

Still, if it is a dream, let us indulge it a moment longer. Let us believe that some things last, and some places and some people are not touched by change. On a fine May morning, with the rooks rising and the hares scampering and the plover calling among the long grass, there is much to encourage the illusion. It is we who change and perish. Parson Woodforde lives on. It is the kings and queens who lie in prison. It is the great towns that are ravaged with anarchy and confusion. But the river Wensum still flows; Mrs. Custance is brought to bed of yet another baby; there is the first swallow of the year. The spring comes, and summer with its hay and strawberries; then autumn, when the walnuts are exceptionally fine though the pears are poor; so we lapse into winter, which is indeed boisterous, but the house, thank God, withstands the storm; and then again there is the first swallow, and Parson Woodforde takes his greyhounds out a-coursing.

UNIVERSITY DAYS

James Thurber

*James Thurber (1894–   ), illustrator, essayist, playwright, bi-
ographer, and general humorist, began his writing career as a journalist in Paris. In 1926, E. B. White got him a job as managing
editor of the* New Yorker, *where he wrote the "Talk of the Town."
With White, Thurber probably did more than anyone else to set
the over-all tone of this magazine. His most recent book,* The
Years with Ross *(1959), is a detailed and amusing account of the
early days of the* New Yorker *and of Harold Ross, the editor of the
magazine.*

*Thurber's sense of humor is most subtle. Often hilarious, occa-
sionally enigmatic, and always clever, he has as well a deep concern
for the position of man in today's world, for the basic frustrations
of contemporary life. As T. S. Eliot said, Thurber's is "a form of
humor which is also a way of saying something serious." Among
his best known works are* My Life and Hard Times *(1933), in
which the following essay appears; the play,* The Male Animal
(1940, with Elliot Nugent); The Thurber Carnival *(1945); and*
The Thirteen Clocks *(1950).*

I passed all the other courses that I took at my University,
but I could never pass botany. This was because all botany
students had to spend several hours a week in a laboratory
looking through a microscope at plant cells, and I could never
see through a microscope. I never once saw a cell through a
microscope. This used to enrage my instructor. He would
wander around the laboratory pleased with the progress all the
students were making in drawing the involved and, so I am
told, interesting structure of flower cells, until he came to me.
I would just be standing there. "I can't see anything," I would

say. He would begin patiently enough, explaining how anybody can see through a microscope, but he would always end up in a fury, claiming that I could *too* see through a microscope but just pretended that I couldn't. "It takes away from the beauty of flowers anyway," I used to tell him. "We are not concerned with beauty in this course," he would say. "We are concerned solely with what I may call the *mechanics* of flars." "Well," I'd say, "I can't see anything." "Try it just once again," he'd say, and I would put my eye to the microscope and see nothing at all, except now and again, a nebulous milky substance—a phenomenon of maladjustment. You were supposed to see a vivid, restless clockwork of sharply defined plant cells. "I see what looks like a lot of milk," I would tell him. This, he claimed, was the result of my not having adjusted the microscope properly; so he would readjust it for me, or rather, for himself. And I would look again and see milk.

I finally took a deferred pass, as they called it, and waited a year and tried again. (You had to pass one of the biological sciences or you couldn't graduate.) The professor had come back from vacation brown as a berry, bright-eyed, and eager to explain cell-structure again to his classes. "Well," he said to me, cheerily, when we met in the first laboratory hour of the semester, "we're going to see cells this time, aren't we?" "Yes, sir," I said. Students to right of me and to left of me and in front of me were seeing cells; what's more, they were quietly drawing pictures of them in their notebooks. Of course, I didn't see anything.

"We'll try it," the professor said to me, grimly, "with every adjustment of the microscope known to man. As God is my witness, I'll arrange this glass so that you see cells through it or I'll give up teaching. In twenty-two years of botany, I—" He cut off abruptly for he was beginning to quiver all over, like Lionel Barrymore, and he genuinely wished to hold onto his temper: his scenes with me had taken a great deal out of him.

So we tried it with every adjustment of the microscope known to man. With only one of them did I see anything but blackness or the familiar lacteal opacity, and that time I saw, to my pleasure and amazement, a variegated constellation of flecks, specks, and dots. These I hastily drew. The instructor, noting my activity, came back from an adjoining desk, a smile on his lips and his eyebrows high in hope. He looked at my cell drawing. "What's that?" he demanded, with a hint of a squeal in his voice. "That's what I saw," I said. "You didn't, you didn't, you *did*n't!" he screamed, losing control of his temper instantly, and he bent over and squinted into the microscope. His head snapped up. "That's your eye!" he shouted. "You've fixed the lens so that it reflects! You've drawn your eye!"

Another course that I didn't like, but somehow managed to pass, was economics. I went to that class straight from the botany class, which didn't help me any in understanding either subject. I used to get them mixed up. But not as mixed up as another student in my economics class who came there direct from a physics laboratory. He was a tackle on the football team, named Bolenciecwcz. At that time Ohio State University had one of the best football teams in the country, and Bolenciecwcz was one of its outstanding stars. In order to be eligible to play it was necessary for him to keep up in his studies, a very difficult matter, for while he was not dumber than an ox he was not any smarter. Most of his professors were lenient and helped him along. None gave him more hints, in answering questions, or asked him simpler ones than the economics professor, a thin, timid man named Bassum. One day when we were on the subject of transportation and distribution, it came Bolenciecwcz's turn to answer a question. "Name one means of transportation," the professor said to him. No light came into the big tackle's eyes. "Just any means of transportation," said the professor. Bolenciecwcz sat staring at him. "That is," pursued the professor, "any medium, agency, or method of going from one place to another." Bolenciecwcz had the look of a man who is being led into a trap. "You may choose among steam, horse-drawn, or electrically propelled vehicles," said the instructor. "I might suggest the one which we commonly take in making long journeys across land." There was a profound silence in which everybody stirred uneasily, including Bolenciecwcz and Mr. Bassum. Mr. Bassum abruptly broke this silence in an amazing manner. "Choo-choo-choo," he said, in a low voice, and turned instantly scarlet. He glanced appealingly around the room. All of us, of course, shared Mr. Bassum's desire that Bolenciecwcz should stay abreast of the class in economics, for the Illinois game, one of the hardest and most important of the season, was only a week off. "Toot, toot, too-tooooooot!" some student with a deep voice moaned; and we all looked encouragingly at Bolenciecwcz. Somebody else gave a fine imitation of a locomotive letting off steam. Mr. Bassum himself rounded off the little show. "Ding, dong, ding, dong," he said, hopefully. Bolenciecwcz was staring at the floor now, trying to think, his great brow furrowed, his huge hands rubbing together, his face red.

"How did you come to college this year, Mr. Bolenciecwcz?" asked the professor. "*Chuffa* chuffa, *chuffa* chuffa."

"M'father sent me," said the football player.

"What on?" asked Bassum.

"I git an 'lowance," said the tackle, in a low husky voice, obviously embarrassed.

"No, no," said Bassum. "Name a means of transportation. What did you *ride* here on?"

"Train," said Bolenciecwcz.

"Quite right," said the professor. "Now, Mr. Nugent, will you tell us—"

If I went through anguish in botany and economics—for different reasons—gymnasium work was even worse. I don't even like to think about it. They wouldn't let you play games or join in the exercises with your glasses on and I couldn't see with mine off. I bumped into professors, horizontal bars, agricultural students, and swinging iron rings. Not being able to see, I could take it but I couldn't dish it out. Also, in order to pass gymnasium (and you had to pass it to graduate) you had to learn to swim if you didn't know how. I didn't like the swimming pool, I didn't like swimming, and I didn't like the swimming instructor, and after all these years I still don't. I never swam but I passed my gym work anyway, by having another student give my gymnasium number (978) and swim across the pool in my place. He was a quiet, amiable blonde youth, number 473, and he would have seen through a microscope for me if we could have got away with it, but we couldn't get away with it. Another thing I didn't like about gymnasium work was that they made you strip the day you registered. It is impossible for me to be happy when I am stripped and being asked a lot of questions. Still, I did better than a lanky agricultural student who was cross-examined just before I was. They asked each student what college he was in—that is, whether Arts, Engineering, Commerce, or Agriculture. "What college are you in?" the instructor snapped at the youth in front of me. "Ohio State University," he said promptly.

It wasn't that agricultural student but it was another a whole lot like him who decided to take up journalism, possibly on the ground that when farming went to hell he could fall back on newspaper work. He didn't realize, of course, that that would be very much like falling back full-length on a kit of carpenter's tools. Haskins didn't seem cut out for journalism, being too embarrassed to talk to anybody and unable to use a typewriter, but the editor of the college paper assigned him to the cow barns, the sheep house, the horse pavilion, and the animal husbandry department generally. This was a genuinely big "beat," for it took up five times as much ground and got ten times as great a legislative appropriation as the College of Liberal Arts. The agricultural student knew animals, but nevertheless his stories were dull and colorlessly written. He took all afternoon on each of them, because he had to hunt for each letter on the typewriter. Once in a while he had to ask somebody to help him hunt. "C" and "L," in particular, were hard letters for him to find. His editor finally got pretty much annoyed at the farmer-journalist because his pieces were so uninteresting. "See here, Haskins," he snapped at him one day, "why is it we never have anything hot from you on the horse pavilion? Here we have two hundred head of horses on this campus—more than any other university in the Western Conference except Purdue—and yet you never get any real lowdown on them. Now shoot over to the horse barns and dig up something lively." Haskins shambled out and came back in about an hour; he said he had something. "Well, start it off snappily," said the editor. "Something people will read." Haskins set to work and in a couple of hours brought a sheet of typewritten paper to the desk; it was a two-hundred word story about some disease that had broken out among the horses. Its opening sentence was simple but arresting. It read: "Who has noticed the sores on the tops of the horses in the animal husbandry building?"

Ohio State was a land grant university and therefore two years of military drill was compulsory. We drilled with old Springfield rifles and studied the tactics of the Civil War even though the World War was going on at the time. At 11 o'clock each morning thousands of freshmen and sophomores used to deploy over the campus, moodily creeping up on the old chemistry building. It was good training for the kind of warfare that was waged at Shiloh but it had no connection with what was going on in Europe. Some people used to think there was German money behind it, but they didn't dare say so or they would have been thrown in jail as German spies. It was a period of muddy thought and marked, I believe, the decline of higher education in the Middle West.

As a soldier I was never any good at all. Most of the cadets were glumly indifferent soldiers, but I was no good at all. Once General Littlefield, who was commandant of the cadet corps, popped up in front of me during regimental drill and snapped, "You are the main trouble with this university!" I think he meant that my type was the main trouble with the university but he may have meant me individually. I was mediocre at drill, certainly—that is, until my senior year. By that time I had drilled longer than anybody else in the Western Conference, having failed at military at the end of each preceding year so that I had to do it all over again. I was the only senior still in uniform. The uniform which, when new, had made me look like an interurban railway conductor, now that it had become faded and too tight made me look like Bert Williams in his bell-boy act. This had a definitely bad effect on my morale. Even so, I had become by sheer practise little short of wonderful at squad manoeuvres.

One day General Littlefield picked our company out of the whole regiment and tried to get it mixed up by putting it through one movement after another as fast as we could execute them: squads right, squads left, squads on right into line, squads right about, squads left front into line, etc. In about three minutes one hundred and nine men were marching in one direction and I was marching away from them at an angle of forty degrees, all alone. "Company, halt!" shouted General Littlefield, "That man is the only man who has it right!" I was made a corporal for my achievement.

The next day General Littlefield summoned me to his office. He was swatting flies when I went in. I was silent and he was silent too, for a long time. I don't think he remembered me or why he had sent for me, but he didn't want to admit it. He swatted some more flies, keeping his eyes on them narrowly before he let go with the swatter. "Button up your coat!" he snapped. Looking back on it now I can see that he meant me although he was looking at a fly, but I just stood there. Another fly came to rest on a paper in front of the general and began rubbing its hind legs together. The general lifted the swatter cautiously. I moved restlessly and the fly flew away. "You startled him!" barked General Littlefield, looking at me severely. I said I was sorry. "That won't help the situation!" snapped the General, with cold military logic. I didn't see what I could do except offer to chase some more flies toward his desk, but I didn't say anything. He stared out the window at the faraway figures of co-eds crossing the campus toward the library. Finally, he told me I could go. So I went. He either didn't know which cadet I was or else he forgot what he wanted to see me about. It may have been that he wished to apologize for having called me the main trouble with the university; or maybe he had decided to compliment me on my brilliant drilling of the day before and then at the last minute decided not to. I don't know. I don't think about it much any more.

ON THE ROAD

Aldous Huxley

Aldous Huxley (1894–   ), grandson of Thomas Huxley and great-nephew of Matthew Arnold, is perhaps best known as the author of such novels as Point Counter Point *(1928) and* Brave New World *(1932). As a writer, he is less concerned with the senses or emotions than with mental attitudes and ideas and with personal, psychological freedom. It is possibly for this reason that his books seem more like collected essays than novels.*

Beyond the Mexique Bay (1934), from which the following essay is taken, records Mr. Huxley's impressions of a trip through Mexico and Central America. "On the Road" shows how travel material which is essentially descriptive may be transformed into something less concerned with sensory impressions than with intellectual and lightly humorous conclusions to be drawn from these impressions.

From Antigua, the road to Lake Atitlán mounts gradually to a rolling plateau. The car bumped slowly across it. Rising high above the intervening mountains, the volcanoes of Agua and Fuego haunted our creeping progress, like the unescapable phantoms of a guilty conscience. Every few miles we would find the table-land slashed across by an immense *barranca*, or ravine. The *barranca* is a Central American speciality. Deep river valleys exist in other parts of the world; but nowhere, at any rate in my experience, are there so many of them and of such inordinate depth as in Guatemala and Mexico. Even on the motorist these horrible gashes in the earth make a disquieting impression. And when you are on mule-back, you come to hate them with a quite extraordinary intensity of passion. You are ambling quietly along, with the church towers of your destination shining on the sky only a mile or two in front of you, when suddenly, without warning, you find yourself at the edge of a *barranca*. A great gulf two or three thousand feet deep divides you from your goal. You pull up your mule and look first wistfully across at the village, so near and yet so horribly distant, on the opposite lip of the ravine; then down into the depths, where the solitary house by the stream is like a toy and the patches of cultivation are laid out as though on the six-inch ordnance map; and finally you examine the track— all those weary loops and hairpins of slithering stones going down to the ford and those still wearier loops and hairpins climbing up on the other side. And at long last, resigning yourself to the inevitable, you spur your mule—that is, if your legs are short enough; my rowelled heels always clanked together under the the the creature's belly—and, standing up in your stirrups to give a momentary respite to your galled buttocks, you let yourself be carried, lurch after lurch, down the break-neck descent into the valley.

Nature worship is a product of good communications. In the seventeenth century all sensible men disliked wild nature. One has only to read Pepys's account of a country tour to understand the reason why. But a change was at hand. During the earlier years of the eighteenth century the French road system was completely overhauled; and from 1725 onwards General Wade was engaged in giving to Scotland and the Border their first decent highways. It began to be possible to look at wild nature in comfort and without serious risk. Poets responded to the invitation of the engineers. Rousseau was contemporary with Trésaguet, the reformer of the French *chaussées*; Wordsworth, with Telford and Macadam. Richard Jefferies was born during the railway boom of the forties, and Meredith wrote his poems when the system then inaugurated was at its highest development. Edward Thomas was working in the early Ford epoch, and Giono lyrically ruminates among the Bugattis and the aeroplanes.

Had you seen the roads before they were made,
You would lift up your hands and bless General Wade.

It is only *after* the making of the roads that people begin to
hold up their hands and bless the country. Untamed, nature
seems not so much divine as sinister, alarming, and, above all,
exasperatingly obstructive. To go hiking across the mountains
when you know that at any moment you can slip down into
the valley and find a good road, with motor buses, and a service
of *wagons-lits*—this is a most delightful pastime. But if you
have to traipse across these same mountains, not on pleasure,
but on business, and for the sufficient reason that there is no
other means of getting where you want to go—why, then, the
case is altered. The sublimities of Nature—and these damned
barrancas are unquestionably sublime—come to be regarded,
not with adoration, but with rage, not as evidences of God's
handiwork, but as booby-traps put in your way by some insuf-
ferably waggish devil. In Central America one learns to understand the classical attitude to nature.

MY WOOD

E. M. Forster

E. M. Forster (1879–   ), eminent but increasingly silent British novelist, is best known for his novels, Howard's End *(1921) and* Passage to India *(1924), and his short story "The Machine Stops." His essays, however, of which many (including the following) are collected in* Abinger Harvest *(1936), reveal the subtlety and quiet humor of his mind and style. "My Wood" expresses his sense of a diminishing realm of nature in the English countryside. Though he speaks lightly of the problem in this essay, it nevertheless represented something poignantly important to him, as it does to so many others. Writing in 1959 of the 1920's, Forster complained: "Then the English countryside, its reality for creative retreat into it, were more plausible than they are today. . . . I don't fret over the changes in the world I grew up in. But I can't handle them." Nevertheless, as this essay shows, Forster is able to handle changes in the world with an annoyance not as great as his humorous acceptance. In its control over emotion, "My Wood" is true to the highest art.*

A few years ago I wrote a book which dealt in part with the difficulties of the English in India. Feeling that they would have had no difficulties in India themselves, the Americans read the book freely. The more they read it the better it made them feel, and a cheque to the author was the result. I bought a wood with the cheque. It is not a large wood—it contains scarcely any trees, and it is intersected, blast it, by a public footpath. Still, it is the first property that I have owned, so it is right that other people should participate in my shame, and should ask themselves, in accents that will vary in horror, this very important question: What is the effect of property upon the character? Don't let's touch economics; the effect of private ownership upon the community as a whole is another question—a more important question, perhaps, but another one. Let's keep to psychology. If you own things, what's their effect on you? What's the effect on me of my wood?

In the first place, it makes me feel heavy. Property does have this effect. Property produces men of weight, and it was a man of weight who failed to get into the Kingdom of Heaven.[1] He was not wicked, that unfortunate millionaire in the parable, he was only stout; he stuck out in front, not to mention behind, and as he wedged himself this way and that in the crystalline entrance and bruised his well-fed flanks, he saw beneath him a comparatively slim camel passing through the eye of a needle and being woven into the robe of God. The Gospels all through couple stoutness and slowness. They point out what is perfectly obvious, yet seldom realized: that if you have a lot of things you cannot move about a lot, that furniture requires dusting, dusters require servants, servants require insurance stamps, and the whole tangle of them makes you think twice before you accept an invitation to dinner or go for a bathe in the Jordan. Sometimes the Gospels proceed further and say with Tolstoy[2] that property is sinful; they approach the difficult ground of asceticism here, where I cannot follow them. But as to the immediate effects of property on people, they just show straightforward logic. It produces men of weight. Men of weight cannot, by definition, move like the lightning from the East unto the West,[3] and the ascent of a fourteen-stone bishop into a pulpit is thus the exact antithesis of the coming of the Son of Man. My wood makes me feel heavy.

In the second place, it makes me feel it ought to be larger.

The other day I heard a twig snap in it. I was annoyed at first, for I thought that someone was blackberrying, and depre-

---

[1] Matthew 19:24.

[2] Leo Nikolayevich Tolstoy (1828–1910), a famous Russian novelist (*War and Peace, Anna Karenina*) and religious and social philosopher. He believed that the possession of property led to crime and violence.

[3] Matthew 24:27.

ciating the value of the undergrowth. On coming nearer, I saw
it was not a man who had trodden on the twig and snapped it,
but a bird, and I felt pleased. My bird. The bird was not
equally pleased. Ignoring the relation between us, it took fright
as soon as it saw the shape of my face, and flew straight over the
boundary hedge into a field, the property of Mrs. Henessy,
where it sat down with a loud squawk. It had become Mrs.
Henessy's bird. Something seemed grossly amiss here, something that would not have occurred had the wood been larger.
I could not afford to buy Mrs. Henessy out, I dared not murder
her, and limitations of this sort beset me on every side. Ahab[4]
did not want that vineyard—he only needed it to round off his
property, preparatory to plotting a new curve—and all the land
around my wood has become necessary to me in order to round
off the wood. A boundary protects. But—poor little thing—
the boundary ought in its turn to be protected. Noises on the
edge of it. Children throw stones. A little more, and then a
little more, until we reach the sea. Happy Canute! Happier
Alexander![5] And after all, why should even the world be the
limit of possession? A rocket containing a Union Jack will, it
is hoped, be shortly fired at the moon. Mars. Sirius. Beyond
which . . . But these immensities ended by saddening me. I
could not suppose that my wood was the destined nucleus of
universal dominion—it is so very small and contains no mineral
wealth beyond the blackberries. Nor was I comforted when
Mrs. Henessy's bird took alarm for the second time and flew
clean away from us all, under the belief that it belonged to
itself.

In the third place, property makes its owner feel that he
ought to do something to it. Yet he isn't sure what. A restless-
ness comes over him, a vague sense that he has a personality to
express—the same sense which, without any vagueness, leads

[4] 1 Kings 21:17-29.
[5] After conquering England, Denmark and Norway, Canute (994–
1035 A.D.) tried to make the ocean tides obey him. He was unsuccessful.
Alexander the Great (356–323 B.C.), after conquering most of the then
known world, is supposed to have lamented that there were no further
worlds to conquer.

the artist to an act of creation. Sometimes I think I will cut down such trees as remain in the wood, at other times I want to fill up the gaps between them with new trees. Both impulses are pretentious and empty. They are not honest movements towards money-making or beauty. They spring from a foolish desire to express myself and from an inability to enjoy what I have got. Creation, property, enjoyment form a sinister trinity in the human mind. Creation and enjoyment are both very, very good, yet they are often unattainable without a material basis, and at such moments property pushes itself in as a substitute, saying, "Accept me instead—I'm good enough for all three." It is not enough. It is, as Shakespeare said of lust, "The expense of spirit in a waste of shame": it is "Before, a joy proposed; behind, a dream." [6] Yet we don't know how to shun it. It is forced on us by our economic system as the alternative to starvation. It is also forced on us by an internal defect in the soul, by the feeling that in property may lie the germs of self-development and of exquisite or heroic deeds. Our life on earth is, and ought to be, material and carnal. But we have not yet learned to manage our materialism and carnality properly; they are still entangled with the desire for ownership, where (in the words of Dante) "Possession is one with loss."

And this brings us to our fourth and final point: the blackberries.

Blackberries are not plentiful in this meagre grove, but they are easily seen from the public footpath which traverses it, and all too easily gathered. Foxgloves, too—people will pull up the foxgloves, and ladies of an educational tendency even grub for toadstools to show them on the Monday in class. Other ladies, less educated, roll down the bracken in the arms of their gentlemen friends. There is paper, there are tins. Pray, does my wood belong to me or doesn't it? And, if it does, should I not own it best by allowing no one else to walk there? There is a wood near Lyme Regis, also cursed by a public footpath, where the owner has not hesitated on this point. He had built high stone walls each side of the path, and has spanned it by bridges, so

[6] Sonnet 129.

that the public circulate like termites while he gorges on the blackberries unseen. He really does own his wood, this able chap. Dives in Hell did pretty well, but the gulf dividing him from Lazarus could be traversed by vision,[7] and nothing traverses it here. And perhaps I shall come to this in time. I shall wall in and fence out until I really taste the sweets of property. Enormously stout, endlessly avaricious, pseudo-creative, intensely selfish, I shall weave upon my forehead the quadruple crown of possession until those nasty Bolshies come and take it off again and thrust me aside into the outer darkness.

[7] Luke 16:19–31.

MY FISHING POND

Stephen Leacock

Stephen Butler Leacock (1869–1944), humorist, historian, essayist, economist, critic, and lecturer, was born in England and emigrated to Canada in 1876. From 1908 to 1936 he was chairman of the Department of Economics and Political Science at McGill University in Montreal. On receiving his Ph.D. from the University of Chicago, Leacock wrote: "The meaning of this degree is that the recipient of instruction is examined for the last time in his life and is pronounced completely full. After this no new ideas can be imparted to him."

But if no new ideas were imparted to him, Leacock certainly attempted to convey his own perceptions. In addition to many volumes of internationally known humorous writings—and he has been called "the most popular humorist in America since Mark Twain"—he wrote a number of serious works on history, economics, sociology, and political science (including one which has become a standard text book in the field), and biographical-critical works on Mark Twain and Charles Dickens.

"My Fishing Pond," which first appeared in the Atlantic, *does not have the wit, the satiric thrust of which Leacock was capable; instead this commentary on human futility and the quality of sport demonstrates his quieter and gentler humor.*

It lies embowered in a little cup of the hills, my fishing pond. I made a last trip to it just as the season ended, when the autumn leaves of its great trees were turning color and rustling down to rest upon the still black water. So steep are the banks, so old and high the trees, that scarcely a puff of wind ever ruffles the surface of the pond. All around, it is as if the world were stilled into silence, and time blended into eternity.

I realized again as I looked at the pond what a beautiful, secluded spot it was, how natural its appeal to the heart of the angler. You turn off a country road, go sideways across a meadow and over a hill, and there it lies—a sheet of still water, with high, high banks, grown with great trees. Long years ago someone built a sawmill, all gone now, at the foot of the valley and threw back the water to make a pond, perhaps a quarter of a mile long. At the widest it must be nearly two hundred feet —the most skillful fisherman may make a full cast both ways. At the top end, where it runs narrow among stumps and rushes, there is no room to cast except with direction and great skill.

Let me say at once, so as to keep no mystery about it, that there are no fish in my pond. So far as I know there never have been. But I have never found that to make any difference. Certainly none to the men I bring there—my chance visitors from the outside world—for an afternoon of casting.

If there are no fish in the pond, at least they never know it. They never doubt it; they never ask, and I let it go at that.

It is well known hereabouts that I do not take anybody and everybody out to my fishpond. I only care to invite people who can really fish, who can cast a line—experts, and especially people from a distance to whom the whole neighborhood is new and attractive, the pond seen for the first time. If I took out ordinary men, especially men near home, they would very likely notice that they got no fish. The expert doesn't. He knows trout fishing too well. He knows that even in a really fine pond, such as he sees mine is, there are days when not a trout will rise. He'll explain it to you himself; and, having explained it, he is all the better pleased if he turns out to be right and they don't rise.

Trout, as everyone knows who is an angler, never rise after a rain, nor before one; it is impossible to get them to rise in the heat; and any chill in the air keeps them down. The absolutely right day is a still, cloudy day, but even then there are certain kinds of clouds that prevent a rising of the trout. Indeed, I have only to say to one of my expert friends, "Queer, they didn't bite!" and he's off to a good start with an explanation. There is such a tremendous lot to know about trout fishing that men who are keen on it can discuss theories of fishing by the hour.

Such theories we generally talk over—my guest of the occasion and I—as we make our preparations at the pond. You see, I keep there all the apparatus that goes with fishing—a punt, with lockers in the sides of it, a neat little dock built out of cedar (cedar attracts the trout), and, best of all, a little shelter house, a quaint little place like a pagoda, close beside the water and yet under the trees. Inside is tackle, all sorts of tackle, hanging round the walls in a mixture of carelessness and order.

"Look, old man," I say, "if you like to try a running paternoster, take this one," or, "Have you ever seen these Japanese leads? No, they're not a gut; they're a sort of floss."

"I doubt if I can land one with that," he says.

"Perhaps not," I answer. In fact, I'm sure he couldn't; there isn't any to land.

On pegs in the pagoda hangs a waterproof mackintosh or two, for you never know—you may be caught in a shower just when the trout are starting to rise. Then, of course, a sort of cellarette cupboard with decanters and bottles, and gingersnaps, and perhaps an odd pot of anchovy paste—no one wants to quit good fishing for mere hunger. Nor does any real angler care to begin fishing without taking just a drop (Just a touch—be careful! Whoa! Whoa!) of something to keep out the cold, or to wish good luck for the chances of the day.

I always find, when I bring out one of my friends, that these mere preparatives or preparations, these preliminaries of angling, are the best part of it. Often they take half an hour. There is so much to discuss—the question of weights of tackle, the color of the fly to use, and broad general questions of theory, such as whether it matters what kind of hat a man wears. It seems that trout will rise for some hats, and for others not. One of my best guests, who has written a whole book on fly fishing, is particularly strong on hats and color. "I don't think I'd wear that hat, old man," he says, "much too dark for a day like this."

"I wore it all last month," I said. "So you might, but that was August. I wouldn't wear a dark hat in September; and that tie is too dark a blue, old man."

So I knew that that made it all right. I kept the hat on. We had a grand afternoon; we got no fish.

I admit that the lack of fish in my pond requires sometimes a little tact in management. The guest gets a little restless. So I say to him, "You certainly have the knack of casting!"—and he gets so absorbed in casting farther and farther that he forgets the fish. Or I take him toward the upper end and he gets his line caught on bulrush—that might be a bite. Or, if he still keeps restless, I say suddenly, "Hush! Was that a fish jumped?" That will silence any true angler instantly. "You stand in the bow," I whisper, "and I'll paddle gently in that direction." It's the *whispering* that does it. We are still a hundred yards away from any trout that could hear us even if a trout were there. But that makes no difference. Some of the men I take out begin to whisper a mile away from the pond and come home whispering.

You see, after all, what with frogs jumping, and catching the line in bulrushes, or pulling up a water-logged chip nearly to the top, they don't really know—my guests don't—whether they have hooked something or not. Indeed, after a little lapse of time, they think they did: they talk of the "big one they lost"— a thing over which any angler gets sentimental in retrospect. "Do you remember," they say to me months later at our club in the city, "that big trout I lost up on your fishpond last summer?" "Indeed I do," I say. "Did you ever get him later on?" "No, never," I answer. (Neither him nor any other.)

Yet the illusion holds good. And besides you never can tell: there *might* be trout in the pond. Why not? After all, why shouldn't there be a trout in the pond? You take a pond like that and there ought to be trout in it!

Whenever the sight of the pond bursts on the eyes of a new guest he stands entranced. "What a wonderful place for trout!" he exclaims. "Isn't it?" I answer. "No wonder you'd get trout in a pond like that." "No wonder at all." "You don't need to stock it at all, I suppose?" "Stock it!" I laughed at the idea. Stock a pond like that! Well, I guess not!

Perhaps one of the best and most alluring touches is fishing out of season—just a day or two after the season has closed. Any fisherman knows how keen is the regret at each expiring season—swallowed up and lost in the glory of the fading autumn. So if a guest turns up just then I say, "I know it's out of season, but I thought you might care to take a run out to the pond anyway and have a look at it." He can't resist. By the time he's in the pagoda and has a couple of small drinks (Careful, not too much! Whoa! Whoa!) he decides there can be no harm in making a cast or two. "I suppose," he says, "you never have any trouble with the inspectors?" "Oh, no," I answer; "they never think of troubling me." And with that we settle down to an afternoon of it. "I'm glad," says the guest at the end, "that they weren't rising. After all, we had just the same fun as if they were."

That's it: illusion! How much of life is like that! It's the *idea* of the thing that counts, not the reality. You don't need fish for fishing, any more than you need partridge for partridge shooting, or gold for gold mining. Just the illusion or expectation.

So I am going back now to the city and to my club, where we shall fish all winter, hooking up big ones, but losing the ones bigger still, hooking two trout at one throw,—three at a throw! —and for me, behind it all, the memory of my fishing pond darkening under the falling leaves. . . . At least it has made my friends happy.

THE SUMMER CATARRH

E. B. White

E[lwyn]. B[rooks]. White (1899–   ), *humorist and poet, is, like Thurber, a graduate of the* New Yorker, *for which he wrote the "Talk of the Town." It is with Thurber that White might be best compared, for they have much in common: an aloof kind of satire, a style whose hallmark is the ridiculous tempered with kindness, a full and supple prose. The major difference lies in the area of concern with man: Thurber is more interested in man and his physical environment, White in man and his social environment.*

"The Summer Catarrh" shows White's ability to use self-ridicule to comment upon man's aspirations and attainments.

Daniel Webster, one of the most eloquent of men, was fifty years old when he first began to suffer from the summer catarrh. I was only six when my first paroxysm came on. Most of Mr. Webster's biographers have ignored the whole subject of hay fever and its effect on the man's career. In my own case, even my close friends possess very slight knowledge of the part which pollinosis plays in my life. I suspect that the matter has never been properly explored.

In May, 1937, the *Yale Journal of Biology & Medicine* published a paper by Creighton Barker called "Daniel Webster and the Hay-Fever." I have just come across it in my files and have reread it with the closest attention. Monday will be the first day of August; at this point in the summer my own fever (which is the early type) is waning. From my study window I can look across to the stubble fields where the hay was cut two weeks ago and can feel the relaxed membrane and general prostration characteristic of the last stages of the disease. Webster, who suffered the autumn type of pollinosis, was in midsummer merely anticipating the approach of trouble. August found him wary, discreet. On August 19, 1851, he wrote to President Fillmore: "I have never had confidence that I should be able to avert entirely the attack of catarrh, but I believe that at least I shall gain so much in general health and strength as to enable me, in some measure, to resist its influence and mitigate its evils. Four days hence is the time for its customary approach."

The four days passed with no ill effects. The fever was late arriving that year. On the evening of the 25th, Mr. Webster took a blue pill, and the following morning a Rochelle powder. The weather was clear and quite cool. Not till the 31st do we find in his correspondence any evidence of distress. Then (writing to Mrs. Blatchford), "Friday about noon: I thought I felt catarrhal symptoms. There was some tendency of defluxion from the nose, the eyes did not feel right, and what was more important, I felt a degree of general depression which belongs to the disease."

Here, in the fading lines of this apprehensive letter, history suddenly grows vivid, and I experience an acute identity with one of the major characters. Webster had had Presidential ambitions, but by this time it had become apparent to him that anyone whose runny nose bore a predictable relationship to the Gregorian calendar was not Presidential timber. He was well past middle life when this depleting truth was borne in on him. I (as I have said before) was a child of six when it became clear to me that a hypersensitivity to the blown dust of weeds and grasses was more than a mere nasal caprice—it was of a piece with destiny.

In 1905, when my parents first discovered in me a catarrhal tendency, hay fever was still almost as mysterious as it was when Mr. Webster was taking his iodate of iron and hydriodate of potash by direction of his physician—who was thinking hard. The first indication I had that I was different from other boys came when I used to go out driving on Sunday afternoons in the surrey. I noticed that every time I rode behind a horse my nose began to run and my eyes grew unbearably itchy. I told my father that it was the smell of the horse that did this thing to me. Father was skeptical. It was a considerable drain on his finances to support a horse at all, and it was going a little far to ask him to believe that the animal had a baleful effect on any member of the family. Nevertheless he was impressed—I looked so queer and I sneezed with such arresting rapidity.

He refused absolutely to admit that his horse smelled different from any other horse, and at first he was disinclined to believe that his son had any peculiarity of the mucosa. But he did call a doctor.

The doctor dismissed the horse and announced that I suffered from "catarrhal trouble." He rocked back and forth in the rocker in my bedroom for about ten minutes in silent thought. Then quickly he arose.

"Douse his head in cold water every morning before breakfast," he said to Mother and departed.

This treatment was carried out, with the aid of a cheap rubber spray, daily for almost two years. I didn't mind it particularly, and except for destroying the natural oil of my hair it did me no harm. The chill, noisy immersion provided a brisk beginning for the day and inoculated me against indolence if not against timothy grass and horse dander.

It was twelve or thirteen years after the Missouri Compromise had temporarily settled the slavery question that Webster had his first attack of the fever. A Whig and an aristocrat, he undoubtedly accepted this sudden defluxion from the nose as a common cold. He was in the prime of life; his youthful ideals had matured; his powers had been demonstrated. He was an ornament to the young republic, when he began to sneeze. Years later, with the ragweed dust of many summers in his veins, he joined Clay in the Compromise of 1850 and heard his own friends vilify him for betraying the cause of humanity and freedom.

How little these critics knew of the true nature of his defection. They said he had his eye on the vote of the South. What could they know of the scourge of an allergic body? Across the long span of the years I feel an extraordinary kinship with this aging statesman, this massive victim of pollinosis whose declining days sanctioned the sort of compromise that is born of local irritation. There is a fraternity of those who have been tried beyond endurance. I am closer to Daniel Webster, almost, than to my own flesh. I am with him in spirit as he journeys up from Washington to Marshfield, in the preposterous hope that the mountain air will fortify and sustain him—to Marshfield, where he will be not just partially but wholly impregnated with ragweed bloom. I am with him as he pours out a pony of whiskey, to ease the nerves. I pour one, too, and together we enjoy the momentary anesthesia of alcohol, an anesthesia we both know from experience is a short-lived blessing, since liquor (particularly grain liquor) finds its way unerringly to the membrane of the nose. I am at his side as he sits down to write another letter to Fillmore. (I understand so well the incomparable itch of eye and nose for which the only relief is to write to the President of the United States.) "I go to Boston today where Mrs. Webster is, and thence immediately to Marshfield. By the process thus far, I have lost flesh, and am not a little reduced. Yesterday and Sunday were exceedingly hot, bright days, and although I did not step out of the house, the heat affected my eyes much after the catarrhal fashion. I resisted the attack, however, by the application of ice."

Ice with a little whiskey poured over it, he neglected to add.

Webster died on October 24, 1852, of liver trouble and dropsy. They did a post-mortem on him and found a well-marked effusion on the arachnoid membrane. It was in the cards that he would never attain to the Presidency; his reaction to flower dust nullified his qualities of leadership. I am sure Webster knew this, in his bones, just as I knew, sneezing in the back seat of the surrey, that I was not destined to achieve my secret goal.

Our lives, Webster's and mine, run curiously parallel. He had an expensive family and expensive tastes—so have I. He liked social life. I do, too. He liked eating and drinking, specially the latter, and was happy on his great farms in Franklin and in Marshfield, whither he turned for sanctuary during the catarrhal season. The fact that he sought the burgeoning countryside in ignorance of what he was doing, while I expose myself wittingly to the aggravation of hay, does not alter the case. Webster lived to align himself on the side of compromise. In time of political strain my own tendency is toward the spineless middle ground. I have the compromising nature of a man who from early childhood has found himself without a pocket handkerchief in a moment of defluxion. Had I lived in slave days, I would have sided with Clay and been reviled by my friends.

It is only half the story. Webster, even though he knew very little about the cause of hay fever, must have found, just as I find, in this strange sensitivity to male dust and earth's fertile attitude a compensatory feeling—a special identification with life's high mystery which in some measure indemnifies us for the violence and humiliation of our comic distress and which makes up for the unfulfillment of our most cherished dream.

SOME THOUGHTS
ON THE COMMON TOAD

George Orwell

George Orwell (1903–1950), novelist, and essayist, had a varied career which took him from India, where he was born, to Burma, France, England, and Spain. His major works, 1984 (1949) and Animal Farm (1945), indicate his leftist political tendencies, but show even more his ultimate distrust of all politicians.

The following essay, which first appeared in The Tribune *(April 12, 1946) shows how the Informal Essay can be used as a form of social criticism while still maintaining the closeness of the author's personality to the material.*

Before the swallow, before the daffodil, and not much later than the snowdrop, the common toad salutes the coming of spring after his own fashion, which is to emerge from a hole in the ground, where he has lain buried since the previous autumn, and crawl as rapidly as possible towards the nearest suitable patch of water. Something—some kind of shudder in the earth, or perhaps merely a rise of a few degrees in the temperature—has told him that it is time to wake up: though a few toads appear to sleep the clock round and misse out a year from time to time—at any rate, I have more than once dug them up, alive and apparently well, in the middle of the summer.

At this period, after his long fast, the toad has a very spiritual look, like a strict Anglo-Catholic towards the end of Lent. His movements are languid but purposeful, his body is shrunken, and by contrast his eyes look abnormally large. This allows one to notice, what one might not at another time, that a toad has about the most beautiful eye of any living creature. It is like gold, or more exactly it is like the golden-colored semi-precious stone which one sometimes sees in signet rings, and which I think is called a chrysoberyl.

For a few days after getting into the water the toad concentrates on building up his strength by eating small insects. Presently he has swollen to his normal size again, and then he goes through a phase of intense sexiness. All he knows, at least if he is a male toad, is that he wants to get his arms round something, and if you offer him a stick, or even your finger, he will cling to it with surprising strength and take a long time to discover that it is not a female toad. Frequently one comes upon shapeless masses of ten or twenty toads rolling over and over in the water, one clinging to another without distinction of sex. By degrees, however, they sort themselves out into couples, with the male duly sitting on the female's back. You can now distinguish males from females, because the male is smaller, darker and sits on top, with his arms tightly clasped round the female's neck. After a day or two the spawn is laid in long strings which wind themselves in and out of the reeds and soon become invisible. A few more weeks, and the water is alive with masses of tiny tadpoles which rapidly grow larger, sprout hind-legs, then forelegs, then shed their tails: and finally, about the middle of the summer, the new generation of toads, smaller than one's thumb-nail but perfect in every particular, crawl out of the water to begin the game anew.

I mention the spawning of the toads because it is one of the phenomena of spring which most deeply appeal to me, and because the toad, unlike the skylark and the primrose, has never had much of a boost from the poets. But I am aware that many people do not like reptiles or amphibians, and I am not suggesting that in order to enjoy the spring you have to take an interest in toads. There are also the crocus, the missel thrush, the cuckoo, the blackthorn, etc. The point is that the pleasures of spring are available to everybody, and cost nothing. Even in the most sordid street the coming of spring will register itself by some sign or other, if it is only a brighter blue between the chimney pots or the vivid green of an elder sprouting on a blitzed site. Indeed it is remarkable how Nature goes on existing unofficially, as it were, in the very heart of London. I have seen a kestrel flying over the Deptford gasworks, and I have heard a first-rate performance by a blackbird in the Euston Road. There must be some hundreds of thousands, if not millions, of birds living inside the four-mile radius,[1] and it is rather a pleasing thought that none of them pays a halfpenny of rent.

As for spring, not even the narrow and gloomy streets round the Bank of England are quite able to exclude it. It comes seeping in everywhere, like one of those new poison gases which pass through all filters. The spring is commonly referred to as "a miracle," and during the past five or six years this worn-out figure of speech has taken on a new lease of life. After the sort of winters we have had to endure recently, the spring does seem miraculous, because it has become gradually harder and harder to believe that it is actually going to happen. Every February since 1940 I have found myself thinking that this time winter is going to be permanent. But Persephone, like the toads, always rises from the dead at about the same moment. Suddenly, towards the end of March, the miracle happens and the decaying slum in which I live is transfigured. Down in the square the sooty privets have turned bright green, the leaves are thickening on the chestnut trees, the daffodils are out, the wallflowers are budding, the policeman's tunic looks positively a pleasant shade of blue, the fishmonger greets his customers with a smile, and even the sparrows are quite a different color, having felt the balminess of the air and nerved themselves to take a bath, their first since last September.

Is it wicked to take a pleasure in spring, and other seasonal changes? To put it more precisely, is it politically reprehensible,

[1] A zone with a radius of four miles, measured from Charing Cross as the center, beyond which taxi rates rise.

while we are all groaning, under the shackles of the capitalist system, to point out that life is frequently more worth living because of a blackbird's song, a yellow elm tree in October, or some other natural phenomenon which does not cost money and does not have what the editors of the Left-wing newspapers call a class angle? There is no doubt that many people think so. I know by experience that a favorable reference to "Nature" in one of my articles is liable to bring me abusive letters, and though the key-word in these letters is usually "sentimental," two ideas seem to be mixed up in them. One is that any pleasure in the actual process of life encourages a sort of political quietism. People, so the thought runs, ought to be discontented, and it is our job to multiply our wants and not simply to increase our enjoyment of the things we have already. The other idea is that this is the age of machines and that to dislike the machine, or even to want to limit its domination, is backward-looking, reactionary, and slightly ridiculous. This is often backed up by the statement that a love of Nature is a foible of urbanized people who have no notion what Nature is really like. Those who really have to deal with the soil, so it is argued, do not love the soil, and do not take the faintest interest in birds or flowers, except from a strictly utilitarian point of view. To love the country one must live in the town, merely taking an occasional week-end ramble at the warmer times of year.

This last idea is demonstrably false. Medieval literature, for instance, including the popular ballards, is full of an almost Georgian[2] enthusiasm for Nature, and the art of agricultural peoples such as the Chinese and Japanese centres always round trees, birds, flowers, rivers, mountains. The other idea seems to me to be wrong in a subtler way. Certainly we ought to be discontented, we ought not simply to find out ways of making the best of a bad job, and yet if we kill all pleasure in the actual process of life, what sort of future are we preparing for ourselves? If a man cannot enjoy the return of spring, why should he be happy in a labor-saving Utopia? What will he do with

[2] A term for the work of poets of the reign (1910–1936) of George V who cultivated the sensational effects of nature imagery.

the leisure that the machine will give him? I have always suspected that if our economic and political problems are ever really solved, life will become simpler instead of more complex, and that the sort of pleasure one gets from finding the first primrose will loom larger than the sort of pleasure one gets from eating an ice to the tune of a Wurlitzer. I think that by retaining one's childhood love of such things as trees, fishes, butterflies and—to return to my first instance—toads, one makes a peaceful and decent future a little more probable, and that by preaching the doctrine that nothing is to be admired except steel and concrete, one merely makes it a little surer that human beings will have no outlet for their surplus energy except in hatred and leader-worship.

At any rate, spring is here, even in London, N.1, and they can't stop you enjoying it. This is a satisfying reflection. How many a time have I stood watching the toads mating, or a pair of hares having a boxing match in the young corn, and thought of all the important persons who would stop me enjoying this if they could. But luckily they can't. So long as you are not actually ill, hungry, frightened or immured in a prison or a holiday camp, spring is still spring. The atom bombs are piling up in the factories, the police are prowling through the cities, the lies are streaming from the loudspeakers, but the earth is still going round the sun, and neither the dictators nor the bureaucrats, deeply as they disapprove of the process, are able to prevent it.

CONVERSATION ABOUT CHRISTMAS

Dylan Thomas

Dylan Thomas (1914–1953), a writer called by Conrad Aiken "a born language lover and language juggler," published his first volume of poetry in 1933. His use of the Welsh idiom, combined with the literary influence of the work of Sigmund Freud, James Joyce, and Gerard Manley Hopkins, and, more immediately, of the rhythms of the King James Bible, quickly made Thomas one of the best known of the modern poets. His three lecture tours in the United States (1950, 1952, 1953) gave rise to the American cult of Thomas-worshipers, who have developed the legend of the man and the poet.

Although his prose writing is not of the same calibre as his poetry, both the short stories and the essays have much of the same exuberance, imagination, "quicksilver wit and high-voltage verbiage" that are found in the best of his poetry. His recollections of his childhood in Wales are earthbound images of a land "lit with the lights of dream" (Louis MacNiece).

The following essay—in an unusual dialogue form—, "Conversation About Christmas," is, in a poetic sense, a better work than its more widely known and often anthologized counterpart, "Memories of Christmas." Here, in "Conversation About Christmas," one comes close to the true, spontaneous throb and fireworks of Dylan Thomas's poetic genius.

SMALL BOY: Years and years ago, when you were a boy . . .

SELF: When there were wolves in Wales, and birds the colour of red-flannel petticoats whisked past the harp-shaped hills, when we sang and wallowed all night and day in caves that smelt like Sunday afternoons in damp front farmhouse parlours, and chased, with the jawbones of deacons, the English and the bears . . .

138

SMALL BOY: You are not so old as Mr. Beynon Number Twenty-Two who can remember when there were no motors. Years and years ago, when you were a boy . . .

SELF: Oh, before the motor even, before the wheel, before the duchess-faced horse, when we rode the daft and happy hills bareback . . .

SMALL BOY: You're not so daft as Mrs. Griffiths up the street, who says she puts her ear under the water in the reservoir and listens to the fish talk Welsh. When you were a boy, what was Christmas like?

SELF: It snowed.

SMALL BOY: It snowed last year, too. I made a snowman and my brother knocked it down and I knocked my brother down and then we had tea.

SELF: But that was not the same snow. Our snow was not only shaken in whitewash buckets down the sky, I think it came shawling out of the ground and swam and drifted out of the arms and hands and bodies of the trees; snow grew overnight on the roofs of the houses like a pure and grandfather moss, minutely ivied the walls, and settled on the postman, opening the gate like a dumb, numb thunderstorm of white, torn Christmas cards.

SMALL BOY: Were there postmen, then, too?

SELF: With sprinkling eyes and wind-cherried noses, on spread, frozen feet they crunched up to the doors and mittened on them manfully. But all that the children could hear was a ringing of bells.

SMALL BOY: You mean that the postmen went rat-a-tat-tat and the doors rang?

SELF: The bells that the children could hear were inside them.

SMALL BOY: I only hear thunder sometimes, never bells.

SELF: There were church bells, too.

SMALL BOY: Inside them?

SELF: No, no, no, in the bat-black, snow-white belfries, tugged by bishops and storks. And they rang their tidings over the bandaged town, over the frozen foam of the powder and ice-cream hills, over the crackling sea. It seemed that all the churches boomed for joy, under my window; and the weather-cocks crew for Christmas, on our fence.

SMALL BOY: Get back to the postmen.

SELF: They were just ordinary postmen, fond of walking, and dogs, and Christmas, and the snow. They knocked on the doors with blue knuckles . . .

SMALL BOY: Ours has got a black knocker . . .

SELF: And then they stood on the white welcome mat in the little, drifted porches, and clapped their hands together, and huffed and puffed, making ghosts with their breath, and jogged from foot to foot like small boys wanting to go out.

SMALL BOY: And then the Presents?

SELF: And then the Presents, after the Christmas box. And the cold postman, with a rose on his button-nose, tingled down the teatray-slithered run of the chilly glinting hill. He went in his ice-bound boots like a man on fish-monger's slabs. He wagged his bag like a frozen camel's hump, dizzily turned the corner on one foot, and, by God, he was gone.

SMALL BOY: Get back to the Presents.

SELF: There were the Useful Presents: engulfing mufflers of the old coach days, and mittens made for giant sloths; zebra scarves of a substance like silky gum that could be tug-o'-warred down to the goloshes; blinding tam-o'-shanters like patchwork tea-cosies, and bunny-scutted busbies and balaclavas for victims of headshrinking tribes; from aunts who always wore wool next to the skin, there were moustached and rasping vests that made you wonder why the aunties had any skin left at all; and once I had a little crocheted nose-bag from an aunt now, alas, no longer whinnying with us. And pictureless books in which small boys, though warned, with quotations, not to, *would* skate on Farmer Garge's pond, and did, and drowned; and books that told me everything about the wasp, except why.

SMALL BOY: Get on to the Useless Presents.

SELF: On Christmas Eve I hung at the foot of my bed Bessie Bunter's black stocking, and always, I said, I would stay awake all the moonlit, snowlit night to hear the roof-alighting reindeer and see the hollied boot descend through the soot. But soon the sand of the snow drifted into my eyes, and, though I stared towards the fireplace and around the flickering room where the black sack-like stocking hung, I was asleep before the chimney trembled and the room was red and white with Christmas. But in the morning, though no snow melted on the bedroom floor, the stocking bulged and brimmed: press it, it squeaked like a mouse-in-a-box; it smelt of tangerine; a furry arm lolled over, like the arm of a kangaroo out of its mother's belly; squeeze it hard in the middle, and something squelched; squeeze it again—squelch again. Look out of the frost-scribbled window: on the great loneliness of the small hill, a blackbird was silent in the snow.

SMALL BOY: Were there any sweets?

SELF: Of course there were sweets. It was the marshmallows that squelched. Hardboileds, toffee, fudge and allsorts, crunches, cracknels, humbugs, glaciers, and marzipan and butterwelsh for the Welsh. And troops of bright tin soldiers who, if they would not fight, could always run. And Snakes-and-Families and Happy Ladders. And Easy Hobbi-Games for Little Engineers, complete with Instructions. Oh, easy for Leonardo! And a whistle to make the dogs bark to wake up the old man next door to make him beat on the wall with his stick to shake our picture off the wall. And a packet of cigarettes: you put one in your mouth and you stood at the corner of the street and you waited for hours, in vain, for an old lady to scold you for smoking a cigarette and then, with a smirk, you ate it. And last of all, in the toe of the stocking, sixpence like a silver corn. And then downstairs for breakfast under the balloons!

SMALL BOY: Were there Uncles, like in our house?

SELF: There are always Uncles at Christmas. The same Uncles. And on Christmas mornings, with dog-disturbing whistle and sugar fags, I would scour the swathed town for the news of the little world, and find always a dead bird by the white Bank or by the deserted swings: perhaps a robin, all but one of his fires out, and that fire still burning on his breast. Men and women wading and scooping back from church or chapel, with taproom noses and wind-smacked cheeks, all albinos, huddled their stiff black jarring feathers against the irreligious snow. Mistletoe hung from the gas in all the front parlours; there was sherry and walnuts and bottled beer and crackers by the dessertspoons; and cats in their fur-abouts watched the fires; and the high-heaped fires crackled and spat, all ready for the chestnuts and the mulling pokers. Some few large men sat in the front parlours, without their collars, Uncles almost certainly, trying their new cigars, holding them out judiciously at arm's-length, returning them to their mouths, coughing, then holding them out again as though waiting for the explosion; and some few small aunts, not wanted in the kitchen, nor anywhere else for that matter, sat on the very edges of their chairs, poised and brittle, afraid to break, like faded cups and saucers. Not many those mornings trod the piling streets: an old man always, fawn-bowlered, yellow gloved, and, at this time of year, with spats of snow, would take his constitutional to the white bowling-green, and back, as he would take it wet or fine on Christmas Day or Doomsday, sometimes two hale young men, with big pipes blazing, no overcoats, and windblown scarves, would trudge, unspeaking, down to the forlorn sea, to work up an appetite, to blow away the fumes, who knows, to walk into the waves until nothing of them was left but the two curling smoke clouds of their inextinguishable briars.

SMALL BOY: Why didn't you go home for Christmas dinner?

SELF: Oh, but I did, I always did. I would be slap dashing home, the gravy smell of the dinners of others, the bird smell, the brandy, the pudding and mince, weaving up my nostrils, when out of a snow clogged side-lane would come a boy the spit of myself, with a pink-tipped cigarette and the violet past of a black eye, cocky as a bullfinch, leering all to himself. I hated him in sight and sound, and would be about to put my dog-whistle to my lips and blow him off the face of Christmas when suddenly he, with a violet wink, put *his* whistle to *his* lips and blew so stridently, so high, so exquisitely loud, that gobbling faces, their cheeks bulged with goose, would press against their tinselled windows, the whole length of the white echoing street.

SMALL BOY: What did you have for Dinner?

SELF: Turkey, and blazing pudding.

SMALL BOY: Was it nice?

SELF: It was not made on earth.

SMALL BOY: What did you do after dinner?

SELF: The Uncles sat in front of the fire, took off their collars, loosened all buttons, put their large moist hands over their watch-chains, groaned a little, and slept. Mothers, aunts, and sisters scuttled to and fro, bearing tureens. The dog was sick. Auntie Beattie had to have three aspirins, but Auntie Hannah, who liked port, stood in the middle of the snow-bound backyard singing like a big-bosomed thrush. I would blow up balloons to see how big they would blow up to; and when they burst, which they all did, the Uncles jumped and rumbled. In the rich and heavy afternoon, the Uncles breathing like dolphins and the snow descending, I would sit in the front room, among festoons and Chinese lanterns, and nibble at dates, and try to make a model man-o'-war, following the Instructions for Little Engineers, and produce what might be mistaken for a sea going tram. And then, at Christmas tea, the recovered Uncles would be jolly over their mince-pies: and the great iced cake loomed in the centre of the table like a marble grave. Auntie Hannah laced her tea with rum, because it was only once a year. And in the evening, there was Music. An uncle played the fiddle, a cousin sang Cherry Ripe, and another uncle sang Drake's Drum. It was very warm in the little house. Auntie Hannah, who had got on to the parsnip wine, sang a song about Rejected Love, and Bleeding Hearts, and Death, and then another in which she said that her Heart was like a Bird's Nest; and then everybody laughed again, and then I went to bed. Looking through my bedroom window, out into the moonlight and the flying, unending, smoke-coloured snow, I could see the lights in the windows of all the other houses on our hill, and hear the music rising from them up the long, steadily falling night. I turned the gas down, I got into bed. I said some words to the close and holy darkness, and then I slept.

SMALL BOY: But it all sounds like an ordinary Christmas.

SELF: It was.

SMALL BOY: But Christmas when you were a boy wasn't any different to Christmas now.

SELF: It was, it was.

SMALL BOY: Why was Christmas different then?

SELF: I mustn't tell you.

SMALL BOY: Why mustn't you tell me? Why is Christmas different for me?

SELF: I mustn't tell you.

SMALL BOY: Why can't Christmas be the same for me as it was for you when you were a boy?

SELF: I mustn't tell you. I mustn't tell you because it is Christmas now.

THE BIRD AND THE MACHINE

Loren C. Eiseley

*Loren C. Eiseley (1907–   ), Chairman of the Department of
Anthropology of the University of Pennsylvania from 1947 till 1959,
and Provost of that university since 1959, is a good example of how
a scholar may, through imagination and a gift with words, make his
subject heard beyond university walls. Through books like* The
Immense Journey *(1957),* Darwin's Century *(1959), and* The
Firmament of Time *(1960), and particularly through essays in*
Harper's, Scientific American, *and elsewhere, he has made anthropology more than a vaguely understood subject. His style—
eloquent, and disturbingly evocative of mysteries beyond man's
comfortably accepted "facts"—is ideally suited to one of the highest
functions of the Informal Essay: that of suggesting universal truths
through an unpretentiously familiar and personal experience.*

I suppose their little bones have years ago been lost among the
stones and winds of those high glacial pastures. I suppose their
feathers blew eventually into the piles of tumbleweed beneath
the straggling cattle fences and rotted there in the mountain
snows, along with dead steers and all the other things that drift
to an end in the corners of the wire. I do not quite know why
I should be thinking of birds over the *New York Times* at
breakfast, particularly the birds of my youth half a continent
away. It is a funny thing what the brain will do with memories
and how it will treasure them and finally bring them into odd
juxtapositions with other things, as though it wanted to make a
design, or get some meaning out of them, whether you want it
or not, or even see it.

It used to seem marvelous to me, but I read now that there are machines that can do these things in a small way, machines that can crawl about like animals, and that it may not be long now until they do more things—maybe even make themselves —I saw that piece in the *Times* just now. And then they will, maybe—well, who knows—but you read about it more and more with no one making any protest, and already they can add better than we and reach up and hear things through the dark and finger the guns over the night sky.

This is the new world that I read about at breakfast. This is the world that confronts me in my biological books and journals, until there are times when I sit quietly in my chair and try to hear the little purr of the cogs in my head and the tubes flaring and dying as the messages go through them and the circuits snap shut or open. This is the great age, make no mistake about it; the robot has been born somewhat appropriately along with the atom bomb, and the brain they say now is just another type of more complicated feedback system. The engineers have its basic principles worked out; it's mechanical, you know; nothing to get superstitious about; and man can always improve on nature once he gets the idea. Well, he's got it all right and that's why, I guess, that I sit here in my chair, with the article crunched in my hand, remembering those two birds and that blue mountain sunlight. There is another magazine article on my desk that reads "Machines Are Getting Smarter Every Day." I don't deny it, but I'll still stick with the birds. It's life I believe in, not machines.

Maybe you don't believe there is any difference. A skeleton is all joints and pulleys, I'll admit. And when man was in his simpler stages of machine building in the eighteenth century, he quickly saw the resemblances. "What," wrote Hobbes, "is the heart but a spring, and the nerves but so many springs, and the joints but so many wheels, giving motion to the whole body?" Tinkering about in their shops it was inevitable in the end that men would see the world as a huge machine "subdivided into an infinite number of lesser machines."

The idea took on with a vengeance. Little automatons

toured the country—dolls controlled by clockwork. Clocks described as little worlds were taken on tours by their designers. They were made up of moving figures, shifting scenes and other remarkable devices. The life of the cell was unknown. Man, whether he was conceived as possessing a soul or not, moved and jerked about like these tiny puppets. A human being thought of himself in terms of his own tools and implements. He had been fashioned like the puppets he produced and was only a more clever model made by a greater designer.

Then in the nineteenth century, the cell was discovered, and the single machine in its turn was found to be the product of millions of infinitesimal machines—the cells. Now, finally, the cell itself dissolves away into an abstract chemical machine— and that into some intangible, inexpressible flow of energy. The secret seems to lurk all about, the wheels get smaller and smaller, and they turn more rapidly, but when you try to seize it the life is gone—and so, by popular definition, some would say that life was never there in the first place. The wheels and the cogs are the secret and we can make them better in time— machines that will run faster and more accurately than real mice to real cheese.

I have no doubt it can be done, though a mouse harvesting seeds on an autumn thistle is to me a fine sight and more complicated, I think, in his multiform activity, than a machine "mouse" running a maze. Also, I like to think of the possible shape of the future brooding in mice, just as it brooded once in a rather ordinary mousy insectivore who became a man. It leaves a nice fine indeterminate sense of wonder that even an electronic brain hasn't got, because you know perfectly well that if the electronic brain changes, it will be because of something man has done to it. But what man will do to himself he doesn't really know. A certain scale of time and a ghostly intangible thing called change are ticking in him. Powers and potentialities like the oak in the seed, or a red and awful ruin. Either way, it's impressive; and the mouse has it, too. Or those birds, I'll never forget those birds—yet before I measured their significance, I learned the lesson of time first of all. I was young then and left alone in a great desert—part of an expedition that had scattered its men over several hundred miles in order to carry on research more effectively. I learned there that time is a series of planes existing superficially in the same universe. The tempo is a human illusion, a subjective clock ticking in our own kind of protoplasm.

As the long months passed, I began to live on the slower planes and to observe more readily what passed for life there. I sauntered, I passed more and more slowly up and down the canyons in the dry baking heat of midsummer. I slumbered for long hours in the shade of huge brown boulders that had gathered in tilted companies out on the flats. I had forgotten the world of men and the world had forgotten me. Now and then I found a skull in the canyons, and these justified my remaining there. I took a serene cold interest in these discoveries. I had come, like many a naturalist before me, to view life with a wary and subdued attention. I had grown to take pleasure in the divested bone.

I sat once on a high ridge that fell away before me into a waste of sand dunes. I sat through hours of a long afternoon. Finally, as I glanced beside my boot an indistinct configuration caught my eye. It was a coiled rattlesnake, a big one. How long he had sat with me I do not know. I had not frightened him. We were both locked in the sleep-walking tempo of the earlier world, baking in the same high air and sunshine. Perhaps he had been there when I came. He slept on as I left, his coils, so ill discerned by me, dissolving once more among the stones and gravel from which I had barely made him out.

Another time I got on a higher ridge, among some tough little wind-warped pines half covered over with sand in a basin-like depression that caught everything carried by the air up to those heights. There were a few thin bones of birds, some cracked shells of indeterminable age, and the knotty fingers of pine roots bulged out of shape from their long and agonizing grasp upon the crevices of the rock. I lay under the pines in the sparse shade and went to sleep once more.

It grew cold finally, for autumn was in the air by then, and the few things that lived thereabouts were sinking down into an even chillier scale of time. In the moments between sleeping and waking I saw the roots about me and slowly, slowly, a foot in what seemed many centuries, I moved my sleep-stiffened hands over the scaling bark and lifted my numbed face after the vanishing sun. I was a great awkward thing of knots and aching limbs, trapped up there in some long, patient endurance that involved the necessity of putting living fingers into rock and by slow, aching expansion bursting those rocks asunder. I suppose, so thin and slow was the time of my pulse by then, that I might have stayed on to drift still deeper into the lower cadences of the frost, or the crystalline life that glistens pebbles, or shines in a snowflake, or dreams in the meteoric iron between the worlds.

It was a dim descent, but time was present in it. Somewhere far down in that scale the notion struck me that one might come the other way. Not many months thereafter I joined some colleagues heading higher into a remote windy tableland where huge bones were reputed to protrude like boulders from the turf. I had drowsed with reptiles and moved with the century-long pulse of trees; now, lethargically, I was climbing back up some invisible ladder of quickening hours. There had been talk of birds in connection with my duties. Birds are intense, fast-living creatures—reptiles, I suppose one might say, that have escaped out of the heavy sleep of time, transformed fairy creatures dancing over sunlit meadows. It is a youthful fancy, no doubt, but because of something that happened up there among the escarpments of that range, it remains with me a life-long impression. I can never bear to see a bird imprisoned.

We came into that valley through the trailing mists of a spring night. It was a place that looked as though it might never have known the foot of man, but our scouts had been ahead of us and we knew all about the abandoned cabin of stone that lay far up on one hillside. It had been built in the land rush of the last century and then lost to the cattlemen again as the marginal soils failed to take to the plow.

There were spots like this all over that country. Lost graves marked by unlettered stones and old corroding rim-fire cartridge cases lying where somebody had made a stand among the boulders that rimmed the valley. They are all that remain of the range wars; the men are under the stones now. I could see our cavalcade winding in and out through the mist below us: torches, the reflection of the truck lights on our collecting tins, and the far-off bumping of a loose dinosaur thigh bone in the bottom of a trailer. I stood on a rock a moment looking down and thinking what it cost in money and equipment to capture the past.

We had, in addition, instructions to lay hands on the present. The word had come through to get them alive—birds, reptiles, anything. A zoo somewhere abroad needed restocking. It was one of those reciprocal matters in which science involves itself. Maybe our museum needed a stray ostrich egg and this was the payoff. Anyhow, my job was to help capture some birds and that was why I was there before the trucks.

The cabin had not been occupied for years. We intended to clean it out and live in it, but there were holes in the roof and the birds had come in and were roosting in the rafters. You could depend on it in a place like this where everything blew away, and even a bird needed some place out of the weather and away from coyotes. A cabin going back to nature in a wild place draws them till they come in, listening at the eaves, I imagine, pecking softly among the shingles till they find a hole and then suddenly the place is theirs and man is forgotten.

Sometimes of late years I find myself thinking the most beautiful sight in the world might be the birds taking over New York after the last man has run away to the hills. I will never live to see it, of course, but I know just how it will sound because I've lived up high and I know the sort of watch birds keep on us. I've listened to sparrows tapping tentatively on the outside of air conditioners when they thought no one was listening, and I know how other birds test the vibrations that come up to them through the television aerials.

"Is he gone?" they ask, and the vibrations come up from below, "Not yet, not yet."

Well, to come back, I got the door open softly and I had the spotlight all ready to turn on and blind whatever birds there were so they couldn't see to get out through the roof. I had a short piece of ladder to put against the far wall where there was a shelf on which I expected to make the biggest haul. I had all the information I needed just like any skilled assassin. I pushed the door open, the hinges squeaking only a little. A bird or two stirred—I could hear them—but nothing flew and there was a faint starlight through the holes in the roof.

I padded across the floor, got the ladder up and the light ready, and slithered up the ladder till my head and arms were over the shelf. Everything was dark as pitch except for the starlight at the little place back of the shelf near the eaves. With the light to blind them, they'd never make it. I had them. I reached my arm carefully over in order to be ready to seize whatever was there and I put the flash on the edge of the shelf where it would stand by itself when I turned it on. That way I'd be able to use both hands.

Everything worked perfectly except for one detail—I didn't know what kind of birds were there. I never thought about it at all, and it wouldn't have mattered if I had. My orders were to get something interesting. I snapped on the flash and sure enough there was a great beating and feathers flying, but instead of my having them, they, or rather he, had me. He had my hand, that is, and for a small hawk not much bigger than my fist he was doing all right. I heard him give one short metallic cry when the light went on and my hand descended on the bird beside him; after that he was busy with his claws and his beak was sunk in my thumb. In the struggle I knocked the lamp over on the shelf, and his mate got her sight back and whisked neatly through the hole in the roof and off among the stars outside. It all happened in fifteen seconds and you might think I would have fallen down the ladder, but no, I had a professional assassin's reputation to keep up, and the bird, of course, made the mistake of thinking the hand was the enemy and not the eyes behind it. He chewed my thumb up pretty effectively and lacerated my hand with his claws, but in the end I got him, having two hands to work with.

He was a sparrow hawk and a fine young male in the prime of life. I was sorry not to catch the pair of them, but as I dripped blood and folded his wings carefully, holding him by the back so he couldn't strike again, I had to admit the two of them might have been more than I could have handled under the circumstances. The little fellow had saved his mate by diverting me, and that was that. He was born to it, and made no outcry now, resting in my hand hopelessly, but peering toward me in the shadows behind the lamp with a fierce, almost indifferent glance. He neither gave nor expected mercy and something out of the high air passed from him to me, stirring a faint embarrassment.

I quit looking into that eye and managed to get my huge carcass with its fist full of prey back down the ladder. I put the bird in a box too small to allow him to injure himself by struggle and walked out to welcome the arriving trucks. It had been a long day, and camp still to make in the darkness. In the morning that bird would be just another episode. He would go back with the bones in the truck to a small cage in a city where he would spend the rest of his life. And a good thing, too. I sucked my aching thumb and spat out some blood. An assassin has to get used to these things. I had a professional reputation to keep up.

In the morning, with the change that comes on suddenly in that high country, the mist that had hovered below us in the valley was gone. The sky was a deep blue, and one could see for miles over the high outcroppings of stone. I was up early and brought the box in which the little hawk was imprisoned out onto the grass where I was building a cage. A wind as cool as a mountain spring ran over the grass and stirred my hair. It was a fine day to be alive. I looked up and all around and at the hole in the cabin roof out of which the other little hawk had fled. There was no sign of her anywhere that I could see.

"Probably in the next county by now," I thought cynically, but before beginning work I decided I'd have a look at my last night's capture.

Secretively, I looked again all around the camp and up and down and opened the box. I got him right out in my hand with his wings folded properly and I was careful not to startle him. He lay limp in my grasp and I could feel his heart pound under the feathers but he only looked beyond me and up.

I saw him look that last look away beyond me into a sky so full of light that I could not follow his gaze. The little breeze flowed over me again, and nearby a mountain aspen shook all its tiny leaves. I suppose I must have had an idea then of what I was going to do, but I never let it come up into consciousness. I just reached over and laid the hawk on the grass.

He lay there a long minute without hope, unmoving, his eyes still fixed on that blue vault above him. It must have been that he already was so far away in heart that he never felt the release from my land. He never even stood. He just lay with his breast against the grass.

In the next second after that long minute he was gone. Like a flicker of light, he had vanished with my eyes full on him, but without actually seeing even a premonitory wing beat. He was gone straight into that towering emptiness of light and crystal that my eyes could scarcely bear to penetrate. For another long moment there was silence. I could not see him. The light was too intense. Then from far up somewhere a cry came ringing down.

I was young then and had seen little of the world, but when I heard that cry my heart turned over. It was not the cry of the hawk I had captured; for, shifting my position against the sun, I was now seeing further up. Straight out of the sun's eye, where she must have been soaring restlessly above us for untold hours, hurtled his mate. And from far up, ringing from peak to peak of the summits over us, came a cry of such unutterable and ecstatic joy that it sounds down across the years and tingles among the cups on my quiet breakfast table.

I saw them both now. He was rising fast to meet her. They met in a great soaring gyre that turned to a whirling circle and a dance of wings. Once more, just once, their two voices, joined in a harsh wild medley of question and response, struck and echoed against the pinnacles of the valley. Then they were gone forever somewhere into those upper regions beyond the eyes of men.

I am older now, and sleep less, and have seen most of what there is to see and am not very much impressed any more, I suppose, by anything. "What Next in the Attributes of Machines?" my morning headline runs. "It Might be the Power to Reproduce Themselves."

I lay the paper down and across my mind a phrase floats insinuatingly: "It does not seem that there is anything in the construction, constituents, or behavior of the human being which it is essentially impossible for science to duplicate and synthesize. On the other hand . . ."

All over the city the cogs in the hard, bright mechanisms have begun to turn. Figures move through computers, names are spelled out, a thoughtful machine selects the fingerprints of a wanted criminal from an array of thousands. In the laboratory an electronic mouse runs swiftly through a maze toward the cheese it can neither taste nor enjoy. On the second run it does better than a living mouse.

"On the other hand . . ." Ah, my mind takes up, on the other hand the machine does not bleed, ache, hang for hours in the empty sky in a torment of hope to learn the fate of another machine, nor does it cry out with joy nor dance in the air with the fierce passion of a bird. Far off, over a distance greater than space, that remote cry from the heart of heaven makes a faint buzzing among my breakfast dishes and passes on and away.

IN THE COMPANY OF CRANKS

Bertrand Russell

Bertrand Russell (1872–   ), *British philosopher, sociologist and essayist, has been one of the most controversial, because he is one of the most individual, men of our age. He has published almost fifty books on education, ethics, philosophy of science, sociology, politics, history of philosophy, and mathematics, and has collected many honors, including the Order of Merit and the Nobel Prize in Literature. In addition to his writing, he operated one of the first progressive schools in England, held a Cambridge fellowship, and taught in several universities in the United States.*

The following essay shows the lucidity of his style as well as his ability to look amusedly at the extremes of nonsense.

I have long been accustomed to being regarded as a crank, and I do not much mind this except when those who so regard me are also cranks, for then they are apt to assume that I must, of course, agree with their particular nostrum. There are those who think that one should only eat nuts. There are those who think that all wisdom is revealed by the Great Pyramid, and among these there are not a few who think that priests carried the wisdom of the Pyramid to Mexico and thus gave rise to the Mayan civilization. I have come across men who think that all matter is composed of atoms which are regular solids having twenty faces. Once, when I was about to begin a lecture tour in America, a man came to me and very earnestly besought me to mention in each lecture that the end of the world would occur before my tour was ended. Then there was the old farmer who thought that all government, both national and local, ought to be abolished because public bodies waste so much

[*Reprinted with the permission of George Allen & Unwin Ltd., publishers, and Bertrand Russell.*]

water. And there was the amiable gentleman who told me that, although he could not alter the past, he could by faith make it different from what it otherwise would have been. He, I regret to say, was sent to prison for a fraudulent balance sheet and found, to his surprise, that the law courts did not take kindly to his application of faith to arithmetic. Then there was the letter sent from a suburb of Boston which informed me that it came from the God Osiris, and gave me his telephone number. It advised me to ring up quickly since He was about to reestablish His reign on earth when the Brotherhood of True Believers would live with Him in bliss, but the rest of mankind would be withered by the fire of His eyes. I must confess that I never answered this letter, but I am still awaiting the dread moment.

There was an incident which illustrates the perils of country life: on a very hot day, in a very remote place, I had plunged into a river in the hopes of getting cool. When I emerged I found a grave and reverent old man standing beside my clothes. While I was getting dry he revealed the purpose of his presence. "You," he said, "in common with the rest of our nation, probably entertain the vulgar error that the English are the lost Ten Tribes. This is not the case. We are only the tribes of Ephraim and Manasseh." His arguments were overwhelming, and I could not escape until I had put on my clothes.

Experience has taught me a technique for dealing with such people. Nowadays when I meet the Ephraim-and-Manasseh devotees I say, "I don't think you've got it quite right. I think the English are Ephraim and the Scotch are Manasseh." On this basis a pleasant and inconclusive argument becomes possible. In like manner, I counter the devotees of the Great Pyramid by adoration of the Sphinx; and the devotee of nuts by pointing out that hazelnuts and walnuts are just as deleterious as other foods and only Brazil nuts should be tolerated by the faithful. But when I was younger I had not yet acquired this technique, with the result that my contacts with cranks were sometimes alarming.

Rather more than thirty years ago, at a time when I shared

a flat in London with a friend, I heard a ring at the bell. My friend happened to be out and I opened the door. I found on the doorstep a man whom I had never seen before, short and bearded, with very mild blue eyes and an air of constant indecision. He was a stranger to me, and the English in which he explained his purpose was very halting.

"I have come," he said, "to consult you on a philosophical question of great importance to me." "Well," I replied, "come in and let us sit down." I offered him a cigarette, which was refused. He sat for a time in silence. I tried various topics, but at first extracted only very brief replies. I made out at last, though with considerable difficulty, what he wanted of me. He informed me that he was a Russian, but not a supporter of the then recent Communist Government. He had, so he told me, frequent mystic visions in which voices urged him to do this or that. He did not know whether such voices deserved respect or were to be regarded as delusions. It had occurred to him that he might obtain guidance from eminent philosophers throughout the world. At the moment it was British philosophers whose advice he was seeking. When he had had such guidance as he could obtain from me he proposed next to consult Arthur Balfour, at that time Foreign Secretary. I listened with such respect as I could command to his revelations from the spirit world, but in my replies to him I remained, for the time being, non-committal. At last he said that he would wish to read some of my books (an extreme step which he had not previously taken) to see whether they contained anything that would be a help to him. For a moment I thought of lending him some book of my own, but I was doubtful whether I should ever see it again and also whether he would really take the trouble to read it. I therefore advised him to go to the British Museum and read such of my books as seemed likely to be helpful. He said he would do so and would return to resume the discussion after he had got a grip on my general outlook.

Sure enough, he came back a few days later. Again I invited him into my study and again I tried to set him at ease. But he looked more dejected and defeated than ever, shabby and hopeless, a drifting waif who seemed almost insubstantial. "Well," I said, "have you been reading my books?" "Only one of them," he replied. I asked which, and found, after some trouble, that it was not a book by me but a skit on my philosophy written to make fun of it. By this time I had begun to think that it did not much matter what he read, so I did not trouble to explain the mistake. I asked, instead, what he thought of the book. "Well," he replied, "there was only one statement in the book that I could understand, and that I did not agree with." "What statement was that?" I asked, expecting that it would have to do with some deep philosophical doctrine. "It was," he replied, "the statement that Julius Caesar is dead." I am accustomed to having my remarks disputed, but this particular remark seemed to me innocuous. "Why did you disagree with that?" I asked in surprise. At this point he underwent a sudden transformation. He had been sitting in an armchair in a melancholy attitude and as though the weight of the world oppressed him, but at this point he leapt up. He drew himself up to his full height, which was five-foot-two. His eyes suddenly ceased to be mild, and flashed fire. In a voice of thunder, he replied: "BECAUSE I AM JULIUS CAESAR!" It dawned upon me suddenly that this had been the purport of the mystic voices and that he was hoping to reestablish the empire which had temporarily been toppled on the Ides of March. Being alone with him, I thought that argument might be dangerous. "That is very remarkable," I said, "and I am sure that Arthur Balfour will be much interested." I coaxed him to the door, and, pointing along the street, said, "That is the way to the Foreign Office."

Whatever Mr. Balfour thought of him when he got to the Foreign Office I never learned, but an obscure footnote to a subsequent new edition of that eminent thinker's "Foundations of Belief" led me to wonder.

KNOXVILLE: SUMMER 1915

James Agee

James Agee (1909–1955) revealed his genius in a number of kinds of writing: verse, essay, novel, film, and dramatic criticism. Both his sense of poetry and his deftness with the evocative essay are displayed in the selection which follows—the opening section of his Pulitzer Prize-winning novel, A Death in the Family *(1957). This passage also indicates that in the most meditative of novels there are sections for which only Informal Essay style is adequate. Like Fielding, Hardy, and Huxley, Agee is a novelist whose bent toward reflective commentary often takes the form of the essay.*

We are talking now of summer evenings in Knoxville, Tennessee in the time that I lived there so successfully disguised to myself as a child. It was a little bit mixed sort of block, fairly solidly lower middle class, with one or two juts apiece on either side of that. The houses corresponded: middle-sized gracefully fretted wood houses built in the late nineties and early nineteen hundreds, with small front and side and more spacious back yards, and trees in the yards, and porches. These were softwooded trees, poplars, tulip trees, cottonwoods. There were fences around one or two of the houses, but mainly the yards ran into each other with only now and then a low hedge that wasn't doing very well. There were few good friends among the grown people, and they were not poor enough for the other sort of intimate acquaintance, but everyone nodded and spoke, and even might talk short times, trivially, and at the two extremes of the general or the particular, and ordinarily nextdoor neighbors talked quite a bit when they happened to

run into each other, and never paid calls. The men were mostly
small businessmen, one or two very modestly executives, one or
two worked with their hands, most of them clerical, and most
of them between thirty and forty-five.

But it is of these evenings, I speak.

Supper was at six and was over by half past. There was still
daylight, shining softly and with a tarnish, like the lining of a
shell; and the carbon lamps lifted at the corners were on in the
light, and the locusts were started, and the fire flies were out,
and a few frogs were flopping in the dewy grass, by the time
the fathers and the children came out. The children ran out
first hell bent and yelling those names by which they were
known; then the fathers sank out leisurely in crossed suspenders,
their collars removed and their necks looking tall and shy. The
mothers stayed back in the kitchen washing and drying, putting
things away, recrossing their traceless footsteps like the lifetime
journeys of bees, measuring out the dry cocoa for breakfast.
When they came out they had taken off their aprons and their
skirts were dampened and they sat in rockers on their porches
quietly.

It is not of the games children play in the evening that I
want to speak now, it is of a contemporaneous atmosphere that
has little to do with them: that of the fathers of families, each
in his space of lawn, his shirt fishlike pale in the unnatural
light and his face nearly anonymous, hosing their lawns. The
hoses were attached at spiggots that stood out of the brick
foundations of the houses. The nozzles were variously set but
usually so there was a long sweet stream of spray, the nozzle
wet in the hand, the water trickling the right forearm and the
peeled-back cuff, and the water whishing out a long loose and
low-curved cone, and so gentle a sound. First an insane noise
of violence in the nozzle, then the still irregular sound of adjustment, then the smoothing into steadiness and a pitch as accurately tuned to the size and style of stream as any violin. So
many qualities of sound out of one hose: so many choral differences out of those several hoses that were in earshot. Out of
any one hose, the almost dead silence of the release, and the

short still arch of the separate big drops, silent as a held breath, and the only noise the flattering noise on leaves and the slapped grass at the fall of each big drop. That, and the intense hiss with the intense stream; that, and that same intensity not growing less but growing more quiet and delicate with the turn of the nozzle, up to that extreme tender whisper when the water was just a wide bell of film. Chiefly, though, the hoses were set much alike, in a compromise between distance and tenderness of spray, (and quite surely a sense of art behind this compromise, and a quiet deep joy, too real to recognize itself), and the sounds therefore were pitched much alike; pointed by the snorting start of a new hose; decorated by some man playful with the nozzle; left empty, like God by the sparrow's fall, when any single one of them desists: and all, though near alike, of various pitch; and in this unison. These sweet pale streamings in the light lift out their pallors and their voices all together, mothers hushing their children, the hushing unnaturally prolonged, the men gentle and silent and each snail-like withdrawn into the quietude of what he singly is doing, the urination of huge children stood loosely military against an invisible wall, and gentle happy and peaceful, tasting the mean goodness of their living like the last of their suppers in their mouths; while the locusts carry on this noise of hoses on their much higher and sharper key. The noise of the locust is dry, and it seems not to be rasped or vibrated but urged from him as if through a small orifice by a breath that can never give out. Also there is never one locust but an illusion of at least a thousand. The noise of each locust is pitched in some classic locust range out of which none of them varies more than two full tones: and yet you seem to hear each locust discrete from all the rest, and there is a long, slow, pulse in their noise, like the scarcely defined arch of a long and high set bridge. They are all around in every tree, so that the noise seems to come from nowhere and everywhere at once, from the whole shell heaven, shivering in your flesh and teasing your eardrums, the boldest of all the sounds of night. And yet it is habitual to summer nights, and is of the great order of noises, like the noises of the sea and of the blood her precocious grand-child, which you realize you are hearing only when you catch yourself listening. Meantime from low in the dark, just outside the swaying horizons of the hoses, conveying always grass in the damp of dew and its strong green-black smear of smell, the regular yet spaced noises of the crickets, each a sweet cold silver noise threenoted, like the slipping each time of three matched links of a small chain.

But the men by now, one by one, have silenced their hoses and drained and coiled them. Now only two, and now only one, is left, and you see only ghostlike shirt with the sleeve garters, and sober mystery of his mild face like the lifted face of large cattle enquiring of your presence in a pitchdark pool of meadow; and now he too is gone; and it has become that time of evening when people sit on their porches, rocking gently and talking gently and watching the street and the standing up into their sphere of possession of the trees, of birds hung havens, hangars. People go by; things go by. A horse, drawing a buggy, breaking his hollow iron music on the asphalt; a loud auto; a quiet auto; people in pairs, not in a hurry, scuffling, switching their weight of aestival body, talking casually, the taste hovering over them of vanilla, strawberry, pasteboard and starched milk, the image upon them of lovers and horsemen, squared with clowns in hueless amber. A street car raising its iron moan; stopping, belling and starting; stertorous; rousing and raising again its iron increasing moan and swimming its gold windows and straw seats on past and past and past, the bleak spark crackling and cursing above it like a small malignant spirit set to dog its tracks; the iron whine rises on rising speed; still risen, faints; halts; the faint stinging bell; rises again, still fainter; fainting, lifting, lifts, faints forgone: forgotten. Now is the night one blue dew.

Now is the night one blue dew, my father has drained, he has coiled the hose.
Low on the length of lawns, a frailing of fire who breathes.
Content, silver, like peeps of light, each cricket makes his comment over and over in the drowned grass.

A cold toad thumpily flounders.

Within the edges of damp shadows of side yards are hovering
children nearly sick with joy of fear, who watch the
unguarding of a telephone pole.

Around white carbon corner lamps bugs of all sizes are lifted
elliptic, solar systems. Big hardshells bruise themselves,
assailant: he is fallen on his back, legs squiggling.

Parents on porches: rock and rock: From damp strings morning
glories: hang their ancient faces.

The dry and exalted noise of the locusts from all the air at once
enchants my eardrums.

On the rough wet grass of the back yard my father and
mother have spread quilts. We all lie there, my mother, my
father, my uncle, my aunt, and I too am lying there. First we
were sitting up, then one of us lay down, and then we all lay
down, on our stomachs, or on our sides, or on our backs, and
they have kept on talking. They are not talking much, and
the talk is quiet, of nothing in particular, of nothing at all in
particular, of nothing at all. The stars are wide and alive, they
seem each like a smile of great sweetness, and they seem very
near. All my people are larger bodies than mine, quiet, with
voices gentle and meaningless like the voices of sleeping birds.
One is an artist, he is living at home. One is a musician, she
is living at home. One is my mother who is good to me. One
is my father who is good to me. By some chance, here they
are, all on this earth; and who shall ever tell the sorrow of being
on this earth, lying, on quilts, on the grass, in a summer evening,
among the sounds of the night. May God bless my people,
my uncle, my aunt, my mother, my good father, oh, remember
them kindly in their time of trouble; and in the hour of their
taking away.

After a little I am taken in and put to bed. Sleep, soft
smiling, draws me unto her: and those receive me, who quietly
treat me, as one familiar and well-beloved in that home: but
will not, oh, will not, not now, not ever; but will not ever tell
me who I am.

PROFESSORIAL TYPES

George G. Williams

George Guion Williams (1902–   ), *professor of English at Rice Institute, has observed the state of higher education from the viewpoint of the faculty member for thirty years. He has concluded that in most cases it is not the inadequacies of the student, but those of the university which create the high rate of failure in today's colleges. These inadequacies involve the faculty, of whom approximately 80 per cent are incompetent; the administration, which is more concerned with efficiency than "delight in learning"; and the over-all organization, which attempts to make students thinking conformists. More conservative readers may assert that Williams is too extravagant, too sweeping in his claims and conclusions; but as B. E. Nelson noted in* Nation, *"[he] may often stroke with too broad a brush and with too vivid a color, but any perceptive student can tell you that his criticisms are legitimate and vital."*

Like all other definitions, the definition of what constitutes a "good professor" must be arbitrary. My own definition would involve the following items, arranged in an ascending order of importance: (1) His students learn well what he teaches them about his subject; (2) his students learn that knowledge and the process of acquiring knowledge are an endless and irresistible source of delight; (3) his students learn to seek, in every circumstance, the best and the highest that lies *within themselves*. By these criteria, hardly one professor in several hundred would receive a grade of A-plus. Not more than one in twenty would receive an A. At least 10 per cent would receive a flat F. Not more than 10 per cent would rate a B. About 30 per cent would deserve a C, and over 40 per cent a D. These estimates are, of course, personal; there are no

[*From George Williams,* Some of My Best Friends Are Professors, *reprinted by permission of Abelard Schuman Ltd. Copyright 1958 by George Williams.*]

statistics. But they are based on nearly forty years of interested observation and experience, and they are (if anything) charitable. (I have just asked three of my nonprofessorial friends for their estimates of their former college professors. Without exception, the three rated the professors lower than I have just rated professors in general.)

Essentially, there is only one type of good professor. He is learned, enthusiastic about learning, original, empathic, innately suspicious of rules and regulations that endeavor to uniformize personalities, more eager to encourage students than to judge them, always conscious that appreciation is ten times more efficient as an educational device than is condemnation. This kind of professor has heartened and saved many a student who otherwise would have been lost; and though the other professors do not ordinarily respect him so much as they do their "tougher" colleagues, he is a kind of university conscience whom they cannot forget, whose existence shames them a little, and whose example influences them subtly even though they resist it. His mere presence on the campus is a continuous reminder (disturbing to the administration and to the other professors) that students are, in spite of IBM cards and efficiency-obsessed administrators, individual human beings. It is unfortunate that this professor is so rare on the campus, and a tragedy that he is becoming rarer.

The "bad" professors are much more various. Maybe this fact is vaguely analogous to a remark made by Dorothy Sayers many years ago, "There is only one way to make love, but there are a thousand ways to commit a murder." There is only one way to be a good professor, but there are at least seven ways to be a bad one. Let me describe these seven types of the bad professor:

Worthy of first mention because he may be a very good man while being a very bad professor, is the plain stupid professor. Again, the ways to be stupid are multiple. The stupid professor may be merely ignorant—trying to teach a subject he doesn't know or understand. Or he may be too stupid to know when he is boring people, or when he is antagonizing them, or when he is amusing them at his own expense, or when he is talking over their heads, or when he is insulting their intelligence. Or he may be too stupid to adapt himself to special conditions in the classroom or about the campus, or to elicit the best from the personalities in his classes. Or his stupidity may manifest itself as an intellectual lethargy, or perhaps obduracy, as suggested in the previous section: he does not want to bother to learn anything new, or to revamp his old ideas to make them consistent with current realities. Most commonly, he is a rule-follower because rule-following simplifies life, and he needs to live a simple life.

The second type is the smug professor—the one with a kind of feline complacency and an imperturbable confidence that he is most clever and most knowing. He has proved to himself that he is a pretty smart fellow. For has he not received excellent grades in college, done successful graduate work, written a learned dissertation, received an accolade of various degrees, and enjoyed regular advancements in his position at the university? Has he not published articles in the learned journals? And by diligent research has he not become undisputed master of some small corner of knowledge? Why should he not consider himself rather good?

Besides, he is daily associated with the immature and poorly informed intellects of his students; and the contrast makes him all the more certain, consciously or subconsciously, about his own intellectual pre-eminence. His wife, in order to bolster her own confidence that she herself was pretty sharp in taking him as a husband, plays up to his concept of himself, and trains the children to do the same. I once heard of a professor's small son whose mother had trained him to repeat several times daily: "Papa is a very great man." Under these conditions, how can the professor avoid becoming smug?

As he grows older, the smug professor becomes elegantly conventional, invariably optimistic, critical of just those things that everybody else criticizes. The apotheosis of worldliness, he associates habitually with only the right people (this equals the wealthy families in the town, and the up-and-coming professors on the campus); he participates with voluble enthusiasm in every "cultural" activity that is supported by the right people in the community; he is liberal in his religious and political views, but never so liberal as to offend the right people; he is eager to assist all students who agree with him and admire him; he disapproves of only the crassly independent mind that dares disturb his universe with a question. This type of professor is everywhere evident in every university.

Fortunately less common (but unfortunately still common enough) is the third type of personality produced by the intellectual obduracy characteristic of professors. This is the arrogant professor. He is never arrogant to those "from whom advancement may befall"; but he is arrogant to everybody else —to students, to graduate students, to faculty members who are his inferiors in the campus hierarchy. Most especially, if he hails from the graduate school of some famous university, he is arrogant to the yokel-like students of his new university. All the unhappiness, hostility, and scorn suffered in the graduate student's and the young instructor's soul, while he underwent the insecurities, uncertainties, deprivations, humilities, and drudgeries of his early days, finds release now that the young man has become a professor, now that the subordinate has become a master.

The rudeness of this professor is incredible. He has not the slightest inkling of what Emerson knew so well—that "the secret of education lies in respecting the pupil." He will interrupt students giving oral reports in class by a continual flow of remarks: "That isn't so at all!"; "Oh, no! You've got that all wrong"; "We've had enough of that. Go sit down!" He will cut students down in class with sarcastic remarks. He will write bludgeoning comments on papers. Here are two illustrative incidents that occurred in my presence this very day:

I happen to pause for a moment in a colleague's office. A student comes to the door and says, "Excuse me, Dr. Blank. But did you get that paper on such-and-such a topic that I laid on your desk yesterday?"

"Oh," says Dr. Blank, "so you're the one that wrote that

paper? I wondered who on earth could have written one so bad!"

An hour later I am walking across the campus with another colleague. A student in one of my advanced courses stops me for a moment to ask a question. My colleague, who knows the young man, says, "What! Are you taking his advanced course? I thought you were damned lucky to get through my freshman course in the same subject!"

Obviously, professors of this type cannot inspire a student with a desire to learn, or love of a subject, or love of a university that harbors such professors. All the student wants to do is to get out of the university, and shuffle off its unpleasant associations as quickly as possible.

In his extreme form this type of professor has a eunuchlike cruelty. Admittedly, the extreme form is not so frequently found; but just one in a department, or even in an entire college, is the one rotten apple that spoils the whole barrel for the student. This professor specializes in the superior stare, the supercilious tone, the calculated trick of allowing a caller to remain standing, the curt and cleverly ironical answer. He likes to make witty and cutting remarks that set everyone present roaring at the victim's expense; he writes ironical "recommendations" that ruin a young instructor's chances of employment; he asks impossible questions on oral examinations, and then acts as if the candidate were a simple idiot for not knowing the answers. All this builds up his own ego, which requires the constant and morbid sacrifice of others if it is to survive.

A much more common, and much less obnoxious, type is the professor who just does not care about people. He likes science or scholarship, books and libraries; he likes learning, and he may even enjoy talking about what he knows. But he has no real human warmth, friendliness, empathy, or understanding of the personalities and points of view of his students or of his colleagues.

I have seen him, as a mathematics professor, lecture to a class of a hundred students with a pipe in his mouth, his back to the class, and his body hiding the formulae he was writing on the board—formulae which he wrote with his right hand while his left hand followed two feet behind with the eraser. I have seen him, as an English professor, leaning on the lectern, reading lectures in a monotone from an enormous pack of little cards which he picked up one by one. I have seen him, as a biology professor, consider a laboratory exercise as an opportunity for him to do some work of his own, dump materials in the sink or on the tables, and disappear for the next four hours while the students tried to make sense out of the hastily and ambiguously written directions he had scribbled on the board at the last minute, and left with them. I have seen him, as a history professor, reading lectures from a loose-leaf notebook, the lectures consisting entirely of excerpts from the textbook which he had already assigned to the class. I have seen him, as a professor of French literature, plowing right onward in his lecture, never pausing to write name of book or author on the blackboard. I have seen him, as an engineering professor, announce to his class of 50 students at the beginning of the term that, no matter what kind of work any of them did in the course, he was going to give 5 A's, 10 B's, 20 C's, 10 D's, and 5 F's.

The mechanical inhumanness of such professors is quite as likely to repel the student as the smugness and the arrogance mentioned earlier. It attracts him to the subject not at all, inspires him not at all, stimulates in him no desire for learning, or love of his university, or respect for the scholarly-scientific-intellectual ideals for which the university should stand. To be sure, this kind of professor may have something to offer a certain 10 per cent of the undergraduates, or twice that percentage of graduate students. But it is difficult to see how these percentages can be reconciled with the truism, repeated ten thousand times, from Jefferson to yesterday, that education for all the people is a necessity if democracy is to survive. A professor who can educate only one tenth, or even one fifth, of his students is hardly serving the cause of democracy—or hardly returning adequate value for all the tax money that is being spent, and the far greater amount that will be spent in the future, in an effort to educate the young people of America.

Just the opposite of this type of professor is the one (usually young) who tries to "pal around" with his students, be their companion and their equal. A product of early solitude and social rejection, he now overcompensates by trying to make his students like him, not respect him—make them value his friendship, not what he can teach them, make them talk about him among themselves as "a real human being," not as a person who instills in them the desire to learn; make them remember him as an agreeable personality, not as an intellectual influence; make them think of him always as a man whom they like, not as a man who taught them something. Though this professor is far from ideal, three things must be said in his favor. First, he is not a negative element in the university as is the intellectually arrogant professor; second, since young people instinctively imitate those whom they like, he may, if he is a real scholar, inadvertently influence his students to want to learn; and third, as he grows older, feels more secure in the world, does not hunger for friendship as he did in his youth, and acquires the dignity of years, he may possibly become the very highest type of teacher—one who can continually maintain an awareness within himself that he is teaching, not masses of names and faces which have little importance compared with the subject he is teaching, but individual human beings whom he is morally obligated to teach—and teach as well as he possibly can.

The next type of professor, though well known and powerful on the campus, is somewhat difficult to describe. Usually he has produced little in the way of published scholarship or science; he is not particularly interested in research; he is not known as a good, or even popular, teacher. But by means of certain stage properties—such as a tweed suit, a pipe, a rather deep voice, a supercultured accent, knowingness about certain backstairs matters in the history of various great professors and celebrated universities, and a peculiar manner of friendly condescension to everybody, he creates about him an atmosphere of urbanity, civilization, culture. He is just a little cynical, yet he is thoroughly optimistic when you get right down to it; he has no real ideas, yet he gives the impression that he could talk about ideas if it were not so boringly uncivilized to be serious in social intercourse; he scoffs gently at convention, yet co-operates perfectly with every convention that really matters on the campus. The trustees, the president of the university, the heads of departments, and the wealthy people of the town are invariably wild with enthusiasm about him. His complacency assures trustees, president, department heads, and citizens that all is well with the university. Any doubts they may have had are gently swept aside by the mere existence of this worldly and cultured gentleman. Disarmingly frank and humorous in criticizing matters of no consequence, he is all the more comforting when he stoutly defends the essential status quo. An excellent man for lulling and suppressing self-analysis and self-criticism.

The last type of professor to be mentioned here is the one who, working within the new vision of education as the output of an administrative "team," and referring to his immediate superior as "the chief," teaches in a supremely businesslike way, with a team of assistants grading papers, a team of stenographers preparing study aids, a team of secretaries keeping records, a team of aids compiling statistics, and a continual effort by all hands to formulate new student-requirements and educational formulae, and to build up local and state-wide committees charged with this or that educational chore. To this professor-turned-executive, the students are so many items to be processed, so many completed jobs to be turned out according to schedule; education is a business, and the student is both the product and the consumer. Uniformity, efficiency, mass production, and mass consumption are the ideals. Absorbed in this dream, the professor-turned-executive loses sight of the student as a human being, a young person whose welfare is the breath of life to his parents, a separate personality whose uniqueness goes unrecognized in the pursuit of administrative efficiency and teamwork.

HOW TO IRON A TELEPHONE BOOK

Fred Dickenson

Fred Dickenson (1909–   ) has commented that he makes his living "sometimes comfortably, often precariously, at writing—newspapers, magazines, a book (mystery novel), public relations, etc." At present, he also writes the continuity for the "Rip Kirby" comic strip.

The following essay which first appeared in the New Yorker, *is an example of the urbane writing for which the magazine is noted. It might well be compared with Thurber's picture of man struggling with the external paraphernalia of life.*

If you have been putting off ironing your telephone book, you need no longer hesitate. I can tell you how it's done. I recently ironed the Manhattan Directory—all eighteen hundred and thirty-six pages. This stimulating adventure had its beginning when our electric dishwasher accidentally turned itself on—a little caprice caused, we later found out, by a short in some inscrutable automatic control. Nobody was home except our beagle, Lucky. There were no dishes or soap in the machine, but these details are really irrelevant. What *is* important is that the top was up. Dishwashers are not supposed to turn themselves on, in the first place, and, in the second place, there are all sorts of safety devices that shut them off when the cover is raised, but apparently a short circuit takes care of this safeguard nonsense easily.

We live in Chappaqua, thirty-two miles north of New York City. My wife was at the supermarket, the children were in school, and I was at my office, in New York, when our dishwasher started automatically flooding the kitchen. When my wife returned home and opened the kitchen door, she was met by a cloud of steam and by the beagle, who, although slightly parboiled, was still able to fly. He set a new dash record from kitchen door to driveway, and vanished under our car.

My wife turned off the machine and settled down at the telephone, first calling the repairman, who said that the dishwasher could not possibly have turned itself on by accident. Then she called me. "The kitchen looks like one of those Kentucky caves" was the picturesque way she put it. "Water is dripping from the ceiling. I never saw so much water in my life. I found a double boiler full of water inside a closed cabinet."

By the time I got home that night, the paper on the kitchen walls and ceiling had dried, leaving only a faint fragrance of old paste, and everything else had been emptied or mopped up. The only important damage was to our precious new 1958–59 Manhattan Telephone Directory. Both the Manhattan and the Westchester telephone books, which nestle on a shelf near the dishwasher (it now sullenly refused to do *anything*), were sopping. I must explain that, as residents of Chappaqua, we are entitled only to the Westchester County book. This, I knew, we could have replaced by simply calling the phone company. But a Manhattan book can only be obtained free in the suburbs by borrowing it from one's own office in the city when nobody is looking, and hauling it all the way home on the train. It had taken me two years to find the exact moment when this nervy maneuver could be executed. And now, within a few weeks, the fruit of my endeavors was a sodden mass.

"Maybe it will dry out by itself," I said hopefully the next morning. "We'll leave it as it is."

A week later, the book had swollen to almost twice its normal size and was threatening to force the phone itself off the shelf. A quick flip—or flop—through the pages showed them to be as wet as ever.

"We'll dry it in the oven," my wife said brightly. "If you can make bricks that way, you certainly ought to be able to

dry a telephone book. I'd say about two hundred and fifty
degrees, so it won't get too well done on the outside."

The oven was turned on, and we slipped the book in tenderly.
Five hours later, you still couldn't get a fork into it. It steamed
merrily but damply, and now we were alarmed to notice that
it was beginning to wrinkle. We took it out and set it on a
window sill to cool.

"There's only one thing to do," my wife said. "We've got
to iron it. How many pages are there?"

I looked. "One thousand eight hundred and thirty-six."

She made a rapid calculation. We have three teen-age daughters. The beagle, of course, could not be counted upon. "That
means three hundred and sixty-seven pages each," she said.

What we did not realize was that teen-age daughters cannot
be counted upon, either, especially when it comes to ironing
telephone books. They simply do not seem to grasp the chal-
lenge. When they came home from school, my wife told them
gaily, "Tonight we are all going to take turns ironing the telephone book!"

They regarded her steadily, with that terrible candor of the
teen-ager, and asked for a repeat. When the full import of her
plan struck home, the response was loud and negative—so negative, in fact, that I, in disgust, said I would do the entire job,
all by myself. I expected a chorus of protests to greet this
suggestion. I was wrong. Ironing is woman's work, but, for
some reason, all the ladies in my family seemed to take the
attitude that ironing a telephone book is a masculine under-
taking, like carpentry or car washing.

Pioneering this little-known field, I believe I picked up a few
pointers that should be passed on to those who may come after.
First of all, when you are ironing a telephone book the size of
the Manhattan Directory, it is important that you be properly
dressed. I chose sneakers, tennis socks, brown chino trousers,
and a T shirt. Although I ironed in the evenings, I found that
even a cool basement laundry room heats up long before you
have completed a hundred pages, and I was grateful that I had

had the foresight to select an outfit that provided maximum comfort and freedom of movement.

The heat dial of the iron should be set for Cotton. Rayon is not hot enough, and Linen is apt to scorch around the edges, particularly if you get to watching for lady chiropractors, Arabian delicatessens, and the like.

Begin at the back. For some reason, it helps to think of yourself as on page 1836, rather than page 1. I will never again see a Manhattan Directory without recalling the ZzzyZzy Ztamp Ztudioz Co., the last entry in the book, and the first your iron touches under the circumstances.

You may sit down while ironing, but only during the earlier stages. I used my workbench stool for a while, but I soon found that as the ironed pages grew higher, it was increasingly difficult to exert sufficient downward pressure to smooth out the more stubborn wrinkles.

Dismiss from your mind any time-saving ideas that may occur to you. It is impossible to iron a wet telephone book quickly and still maintain a high standard of workmanship. There is no use trying to iron more than one page at a time. Purely in the interests of science, and not because of any weakening in my resolve, I tried this short cut as early as the "T"s, taking first four pages, then three, and finally settling for two, but the bottom one will not dry. (In the course of this experiment, I kept the iron on one page too long, and was warned just in time by a tiny spiral of smoke. A half column of Thompsons in my book are now the color of toast.)

And don't think you can speed things up by holding the wet pages in one hand and flipping them down one by one, as needed. It won't work. The moisture causes the pages to stick together, and they have to be separated, with both hands, which means, of course, that you have to put the iron down nine hundred and eighteen times.

For one wild moment, along about the mid-"O"s, I considered using the mangle (*"They laughed when I sat down at the mangle, but . . ."*), and I did take a brief respite to study the machine. You operate a mangle with your knees, of course, and this would have been a welcome change, for my hand had begun to cramp around the handle of the iron. However, it was obvious that I would have to hold the book, feed in one page at a time, and release the roller at precisely the right instant. The danger of tearing the pages was too great, and I went back to hand labor, comforting myself with the thought that the best places always advertise that type of work.

Since there are no short cuts to success in this rather special field, I suggest that you allow at least two nights for the job. I ended my first ironing session around 2 A.M. The next evening was almost a complete loss. Just as I was starting on the "K"s, some friends asked us over, and my wife was too embarrassed—as well she might have been—to say that we couldn't go because I was down in the cellar ironing the telephone book. The upshot was that I had to change out of my ironing costume and play games for the rest of the evening. I finally finished the job at one-fifteen the following night.

Ironing the Manhattan Directory is not mentally stimulating. From time to time, my wife would come down to see how I was doing, or one of the children would call down the stairs to ask me for information about ancient Egyptian civilization. The dog also came to visit, nervously sniffing the unusual mixture of steam, paper, and ink. But even with occasional visitors the hours do not fly by, and I suggest that you try to think of yourself as on a scenic tour of the glittering metropolis. On my magic iron, I glided through the West Side Zuckermans, passed the Yale Club and the Woolworth Bldg., and appreciated for the first time the sprawling bureaucracy of the United States Government—"WEATHER BUR." through "ADVISORY GROUP ON ELECTRON TUBES." There was the United Nations (Yugoslavia through Afghanistan), Trinity Church, the Stork Club, the Smiths (seven and a half pages of them), and the Original Crispy Pizza Crust Co. My iron smoothed the furrowed brows of Merrill Lynch Pierce Fenner & Smith, paused at Luchow's, pressed on to the Joneses (only four pages of them), and dropped into El Morocco for a nightcap. The whole vast panorama of Manhattan (smelling only slightly of hot paper) passed before me, until finally I ironed the last wrinkle from Page 1—"Emergency Calls."

A cautionary note: When ironing a telephone book, you will find that several beers not only enhance the tour but also diminish the importance of any little burns or muscular aches picked up along the way. The quantity of beer consumed must be carefully regulated. I erred on the side of generosity the first evening, and by the time I reached the "Mc"s, I noticed that the quality of my work had deteriorated. In fact, I had to sprinkle the "McD"s and iron them all over again.

THE TALK OF THE TOWN

The New Yorker

"The Talk of the Town" was first written for the New Yorker *by E. B. White and, later, by James Thurber. These two men set a tone for the column—and the magazine—which is still in effect. The column consists of a number of short, unsigned commentaries upon current events, written in a sophisticated and urbane style which is the epitome of good "slick" writing. The commentary is like a miniature Informal Essay, displaying less, perhaps, the personality of its author than the personality of the magazine itself.*

Notes and Comment · January 17, 1959

A man we know went out to the other end of Long Island recently to sell a place he has there, and came back without selling it. When we saw him, he said he had gone to the house to have a last look around before he clinched the deal, and, on opening the gate, had been greeted by two bull calves, which the dairy farmer across the road had turned onto his lawn to graze and to keep the land in heart—an exchange of services that had been going on for quite a time. "The two calves were at a stage I had never before noticed in the male cow," our friend, a city fellow, said. "I always thought of calves as awkward, and bulls as big and mean. These were only about a foot higher than a Great Dane, but quite a lot heavier, and spotted black and white, and they were nimble. They circled me at a distance wherever I walked, bounding in arcs like porpoises going around a ship. I walked back to the rail fence that divides my front lawn from my pasture. My neighbor ordinarily uses that for his cattle, too, but he had no cows in it the other day—growing a winter crop of some kind of grass, I suppose. I leaned on the fence looking across the land, which is pretty but has never really been of any use to me—too far from town, and I'm not a farmer, anyway. One of the calves came up behind me and gave me a nudge, just to show what he could do if he wanted to. I whipped around, and he was out of hitting range, but ready to counter if I wanted to make anything out of it. Balanced on his feet, head down but one eye rolling up to keep me in view. No pawing the ground blindly. When he saw I wasn't mad, he ran away laughing. It made me think. These brave bulls that are killed in the ring are bred to be suckers, from full brothers of bulls that have died bravely. 'Brave' means to charge where there is motion. The calves are encouraged to do the same thing. It's like breeding from boxers who can't keep a left out of their puss, and then teaching the kids to drop their shoulder. [Our man's vocabulary contains a variety of incongruous pigments, which sometimes run together.] I decided to hang on to the place, and develop a strain of bulls to lick bullfighters. What the sport lacks now is competition. Can you imagine a baseball league where the team in the cellar didn't win one in three?"

We shook our head, and he went right on: "Conditioning is important. First, I'll hire a guy to teach the calves to stay away from the moving cape. It should be simple. All he will need is a boxing glove loaded with tea foil under the cape. He waves the cape, the calf charges, and, boom, he hits the calf in the nose. A calf of the intelligence of even the class of fighters on television will learn to work toward his sparring partner's left, away from the cape. He will gallop around in circles until the guy is dizzy, and then get him, the way the calf got me. It seems to be instinctive with a bull calf of normal I.Q. The matadors I've seen pictures of—their legs are gone. I don't think they jump enough rope. They could never meet that kind of attack. I wouldn't try to do it in one generation—maybe not even in two. I'd breed from the bulls that wouldn't follow a feint and that had the best footwork—the cuties. About the third generation, I'd start matching my bulls with a six-round class of bullfighter, who would maybe get a feature *corrida* only in the Spanish equivalent of West Hartford. After my bulls ran up a record, I would parlay one of them against the three greatest bullfighters in the world—I don't remember the names, but say, for argument, El Gazpacho, El Aficionado, and Tome Coca-Cola. The first two names I made up, but I happen to know that the third is genuine; I saw it painted all over the outside of a bull ring in Mexico. My bulls would kill every bullfighter in the world."

"What have you got against bullfighters?" we asked.

"Nothing," he said, "but it would stop an awful lot of bad writing."

Notes and Comment · June 13, 1959

The opening of the renovated monkey house at the Bronx Zoo on Wednesday, May 27th, ushered in the most glorious week in simian history. There was something supernatural about the Zoo's foreshadowing of the triumph of Able and Baker; it could not have been mere coincidence, and the Duke University researchers into extrasensory tarradiddle will be deep into it by now if they have any sense of the marvellous. At any rate, Thursday morning's *Times* and *Herald Tribune* carried pictures of Otto, a *Perodicticus potto*, which is not quite a monkey, but almost, gnawing his way through a marshmallow-soldered ribbon that was stretched across the entrance to the building. Otto was pictured in the arms of Fairfield Osborn, president of the New York Zoological Society and a *Homo sapiens*. Pottos are between lemurs and monkeys on what zoologists call the primate tree, while the regular inhabitants of the monkey house fit in somewhere between Otto and Mr. Osborn; it was a nice touch of educational symbolism.

That midday, still psychically attuned to the reception of intelligence about monkeys, we were returning to our office from lunch when we caught the afternoon headlines on a newsstand: "MONKEYS ALIVE!" (*Post*), "MONKEYS SUR-VIVE RIDE INTO SPACE" (*Journal-American*), "U.S. RE-

COVERS 2 MONKEYS AFTER 1500-MI. SPACE TRIP"
(*World-Telegram*). "Da monkeys done it!" the news vender
cried out to us; there has not been so much jubilant free
communication between strangers in the streets in months.
The headlines, as we all know, referred to the journey to a
height of three hundred miles that had just been accomplished
by Able and Baker, packed in the nose cone of a Jupiter missile,
and when we bought a paper and began to read, it gave us a
chauvinistic thrill to learn that Baker, who rode in the smaller
compartment, was a squirrel monkey. Years ago, we once owned
a squirrel monkey, whose low opinion of us so depressed us
that we had to give him away. (We have learned since that
the verdict of a squirrel monkey need not be accepted in such
cases; although he has an enormous brain box in proportion to
his volume, he has a low I.Q. for a monkey.) Reading about
Baker's achievement produced the same kind of psychological
switch that occurs when you learn that a boy you couldn't
stand in school has become a United States senator or a pitcher
in the big leagues. For the first time, we felt in personal touch
with the space program. (It was obvious to us that Able, the
rhesus, had been merely crew; Baker had been the pilot.)

We had never got on good enough terms with our own
squirrel monkey to address him by a first name. He arrived in
the summer of 1937 by courtesy of the press agent of a vast
combination night club and music hall called the French
Casino, which in those days stood at Fiftieth Street and
Seventh Avenue. The French Casino had a show featuring a
trained chimpanzee, and the press agent sent out a squirrel
monkey, in a small wooden cage, to everybody he thought was
likely to write a line about the new production. Ours was a
male, and so handsome that we decided to keep him. He
weighed about as much as a squab, and had a memorable tail.
We bought him a big cage and fed him on luxury tidbits and
pullet eggs. When we offered him a hand, he bit it. The
trouble was that he knew we had no right to hold him against
his will. He continually demanded habeas corpus. When we
let him out for a bit of exercise, carefully closing the bathroom

door behind the two of us, he would go up atop the shower curtain and not come down until we knocked him off his perch with a wet, rolled-up washrag. We always caught him before he hit the floor, but he didn't appreciate the attention. No kindness in the way of cherries or baby noises could mitigate his indignation. He knew his rights; he was being illegally detained. When we sat home with him in the evenings, he would look at us steadily and shake his head from side to side. "Ts-ts-ts," he would say, implying clearly that we would never amount to anything. We gave him away because we found ourself beginning to believe him. Still, we realize now, it was a fruitful experience. It was the nearest we would ever come to knowing a space man.

Notes and Comment · June 27, 1959

An overloaded peg in the department of ready-made American humor is the back-seat driver. In our experience, it is usually the man at the wheel, and particularly the professional, who talks his passengers deaf, dumb, and blind. The way it works a good deal of the time is that the driver directs a steady stream of gab at the members of the captive audience behind him, while they, progressively alarmed at the revelation of what kind of mind is guiding them, carefully refrain from any answers that might distract him further. "To be in the driver's seat" is an idiom for being boss; there is an almost irresistible tendency on the part of drivers to confuse idiom with reality. (It is our impression that a driver invented this idiom.) The driver can move his passengers where he will—into the adjoining traffic lane or into the rear end of the car in front. This sometimes makes him feel that he can also tell his passengers where to get off.

We have never encountered a taxi-driver who could not inform us, on request, exactly how to solve New York's traffic problem; half of the drivers we ride with tell us without any request at all. This means that we hear the solution on an average of once a day. The first thing to do, they all say, is to get the buses off the streets; the second, to make private cars stay outside the city limits. It has always seemed rude to remind them that this would leave taxis as the only form of surface transportation; it would be like accusing a doctor of wanting to make money. As for the drivers who wait outside race-courses to ferry passengers back to town (with no reduction in fare for the fellow who has to sit on the crack between the jump seats), we have never ridden behind one who hadn't fancied every winner, or who explained why he hadn't backed any winner. And there is a breed of hire-car drivers who, when there is a big fight coming on, are chartered by the promoters to take boxing writers to and from the training camps, out where the air is reputed salubrious. These drivers always know more about fights than any of the reporters who have covered them, or even than the old fighters who ride sadly out to the camps to give their "opinions" of the principals to the press and collect a free meal for the favor. We once rode back to Manhattan with a Boxing Commission physician and a driver who strayed from his own field to the etiology of heart diseases. The driver weighed about a seventh of a ton and had carefully collected case histories of thin colleagues who died abruptly at the wheel, precipitating disasters. The tag line of each history was "He was as skinny as a rail." For the last thirty miles of the journey in, he told us about total abstainers he had known who died horribly from diseases usually associated with heavy drinking. The doctor said nothing.

The feeling of authority associated with driving is not confined to professionals, although they are the most susceptible to its inroads. (In Nimrod's England, stagecoach drivers were notoriously overarticulate.) Hundreds of marriages break up when couples including only one driver move into suburbs where a car is a necessity. Even the most dependent wives, if they drive, become arrogant under such circumstances; husbands who have been only normally bossy become completely intolerable when they are the sole drivers. In situations where the previously dominant personality is the non-driver, divorce is a dead certainty. Learning to drive is no good; the apprenticeship only confirms and embitters the discrepancy. When husband and wife both drive well, life together is complicated by an additional rivalry. When they both drive badly, they blame their mistakes on each other. Having individual cars destroys togetherness; the vacant seat at the driver's right invites intrusions.

We have long considered it fortunate that the isolation of the pilot's compartment in airliners prevents him from bending your ear, but we have noted, with distress, the increasing frequency of announcements over the public-address system: "This is Captain Canyon speaking; we are now passing over Dayton, Ohio," and the rest of it. All we want to know is when we are going to fall, and how far.

Skyjector · March 12, 1960

Madison Avenue, not content with its vast terrestrial kingdom —newspapers, magazines, radio, TV, billboards, subways, sides of buses, and so on—may be about to invade the heavens. This fearful conquest has been made possible by a device called a Skyjector, which is a latter-day magic lantern capable of projecting advertising matter of practically any kind onto clouds at night, ideally at a height of from fifteen hundred feet to two miles and on such a scale that a box of Wheaties might well measure hundreds of feet across and a couple of thousand feet high. The owner of the Skyjector is a Swiss engineer, industrialist, and financier named Michael Schwabacher, with whom we had a talk some nights ago, shortly before a demonstration of the awful powers of his machine. Our talk took place on a windy, desolate corner of Coenties Slip, where we found the Skyjector, resembling a bright-yellow cannon fifteen feet long, mounted on a truck and looking only too ready for action. Mr. Schwabacher is a tall, dark young man of thirty or so, affable by nature but on the occasion of our meeting rather annoyed by New York's weather. "This miserable, fickle climate!" he exclaimed. "All afternoon the sky was delightfully overcast— great fat clouds everywhere, absolutely perfect for our Skyjector. Now look at it! Not a cloud in the sky! Since we brought the Skyjector to New York, we've given four public demonstrations and, thanks to the curse of clear skies, they've all been flops. A while ago, we tried to show off the Skyjector from a parking lot on Sixth Avenue. No clouds, so we had to beam it at the side of the Esso Building instead. How humiliating! To make matters worse, the police came and chased us away as a public nuisance."

Schwabacher glared at the stars above the lonely Slip. To distract him, we asked to hear the genesis of the yellow cannon. "Sheer inspiration," he replied. "I've lived in America on and off for ten years, and there's something about life here that expands your horizons. You think big. For a long time, I'd nursed a grudge against the more traditional forms of advertising—the billboards and garish neon signs that litter your beautiful countryside. I thought what a boon it would be if I could develop a device that would project ads in the skies—something that would catch the eye, yet have genuine aesthetic appeal. In Switzerland, I happened to run into an old acquaintance, an inventor named Fernand Auberson, and it turned out he'd been working on just the sort of machine I'd imagined, but he hadn't been able to find financial backing. I told him to go ahead and design the machine, and leave the rest to me. Last year, while it was being built, in Zurich, the Unexcelled Chemical Corporation here heard about it. Now Unexcelled has an option to buy it from me for around a million and a half dollars. The plan is to send the Skyjector on a tour of some fifty major cities. We hope to line up four or five national clients who'll pay as much as a million a year for its services. On a short-term basis, rates to clients will run about three thousand dollars a night. Of course, we'll leave room for local ads, like for movie theatres and restaurants, and they'll be even cheaper."

We hinted that many people might think there was little to choose aesthetically between the Skyjector and billboards, and that other people might consider defacing the night skies a far worse crime than defacing roadsides. "It would certainly be a shame if the Skyjector fell into the wrong hands," Mr. Schwabacher said. "The Unexcelled people are aware that it must be used most conservatively. A big gambling casino out in Nevada wanted to advertise with us, but we turned it down."

When we asked for a comparison between skywriting and Skyjecting, Schwabacher said there isn't any. "In skywriting, it costs nearly three thousand dollars to get a brand name in the sky, and before it's finished—poof! Half of it's gone with the wind. Skyjection is to skywriting as CinemaScope is to the nickelodeon peepshow. Besides, we're not limited to the sky. We can also project against cliffs, dams, and any other broad surface. You should see Skyjection in the Alps—breathtaking! On a good night, Skyjector can toss a picture as far as five miles, magnifying the original image over twenty-five million times. Our light source, which is still a secret, gets its power from a diesel generator-trailer attached to our truck and is the most powerful ever devised by man—greater than the combined strength of seventy giant searchlights. An adequate cooling system was our biggest engineering headache. The temperature at the light source is better than ten thousand degrees Fahrenheit, and steel itself melts at about twenty-five hundred degrees."

At that moment, a man on the truck called out, "Clouds! To the west! Coming from Jersey!" We looked westward, and, sure enough, a clutter of clouds came scudding over the rooftops. The generator back of the cannon uttered a roar, the pavement of the Slip shuddered underfoot, and as the clouds passed above us a brilliant shaft of light struck them, dazzling our eyes. We blinked hard, and there in the heavens was Brigitte Bardot, followed in rapid succession by Donald Duck, Popeye, George Washington, and the words "PEPSI-COLA" and "PEACE."

We confessed to being stunned. "That was nothing," Schwabacher said as the last of the clouds slipped from sight beyond the East River and the Skyjector was switched off. "In a little while, we won't have to wait around this way for clouds. We'll have an emergency unit on hand to manufacture them—

pink, fluffy clouds—out of helium and plastic particles, superior in most respects to the real thing. Moreover, we've a Skyjector in the works that will be able to operate on clouds in the daytime, by using a combination of infra-red and infra-blue refraction. By next year, it's not too much to hope that we'll be showing motion pictures in full color, in broad daylight, on artificial clouds. Think of that!"

We said, as politely as possible, that we couldn't bear to.

We still can't.

Notes and Comment · April 9, 1960

We have been following with particular interest the efforts of the New York Telephone Company to persuade some four hundred thousand shy subscribers to put their names in the directory. A passion for anonymity, it seems, has currently seized one of every nine local telephonists, and is spreading at such a rate that the company fearfully anticipates a time when only two out of three customers will consent to be listed. To curb this (to it) deplorable trend, the firm has lately begun charging its recluses fifty cents a month just for the privilege of reclusion. The additional fee, it is hoped, will discourage the merely frivolous hermits without working any great hardship on people for whom an unlisted number is, as one executive sternly put it, "a real necessity."

We can understand the firm's distress, and are sorry about it. Apparently, it takes the information operator three times as long to convince a caller that an unlisted number is indeed anonymous as it does to read off an ordinary published number, and the company hasn't got all day. Still, we can't help wondering about the phrase "a real necessity." We seem to detect a note of impatience in it—the specialist's impatience with laymen who obstruct the smooth pursuit of his occupation. This professional view was prettily expressed by the executive who pointed out that "nonpublished numbers are interfering more and more with one of the company's basic functions—interconnecting the customers it serves." One gathers that in

188 THE NEW YORKER

this gentleman's opinion interconnection is a good thing in itself, even if the caller should be an encyclopedia salesman and the recipient of the call a wet, angry man in a bath towel.

It strikes us as no more than natural that the parishioners of the Telephone Company should look upon their instruments with a comparatively temperate enthusiasm. Keeping one's number out of the book is a simple and effective way to insure that one's telephone will be a convenience, and not an intrusion. A man advances more cheerfully to find out for whom the little bell tolls when he is confident that the toller is a friend. Everything considered, and with all respect to the Telephone Company, we regard it as an encouraging sign that four hundred thousand New Yorkers have determined to keep at least one gadget under wholesome discipline. We hope that the company will rest content with its $2,400,000 of extra yearly revenue, and not press the matter further. We can assure it that further pressure will accomplish nothing. Resourceful hermits will almost certainly follow the example of an old industry-baiter of our acquaintance who has got around the new edict by listing his number under a gaudy and imaginative *nom de phone*. Should the company prove relentless, it may yet see the day when its directory will qualify as a work of fiction.